What People Are Saying

"The work that [Dwayne] does and the vision that he has for youth is much needed for such a time as this, especially in the city of Chicago. His pursuit to equip youth in every area of their lives for success is relentless! Dedication is one of his strengths as well as his ability to effectively communicate a message that inspires through the book *The Passage*. The messages in *The Passage* are relevant and personal, to help youth deal with real-life issues, delivered through 'real talk'!...My children and I are forever supporters of Dwayne and his endeavors..."

—Tasha Sykes

"[Dwayne's] passion, heart, compassion, resourcefulness, professionalism, and commanding presence are SECOND TO NONE. It is rare that you still meet a leader who develops teens with intentionality. The inspiration from Dwayne's life and *The Passage* book has impacted my life, and I know it will impact the lives of countless others. It has been my esteemed pleasure to know Dwayne and work with him to change the world, one teen at a time."

—Cicely V. Wilson

"After reading the beginning chapter of *The Passage*, it captivated me and prepared me to break all negative self-talk, to position my heart, mind, and soul to receive practical elements on how to find and live on purpose. It is a must-read for anyone who is searching for their purpose, redefining their purpose, or affirming their purpose."

—Shameka Jones

"Mr. T. Dwayne Smith is the one person who has significantly influenced my life…This gentleman has been my mentor since middle school. He is committed to changing the world, one teen at a time, by offering programs and books that equip and encourage. *The Passage* book has made a tremendous impact on my life, and it has challenged me to see beyond my limitations and circumstances and to create the future I want for my life. This book has given me guidance and motivation to pursue success."

—Joshua Simmons

"T. Dwayne has been a powerful and committed servant…and has lived according to His purpose. He is the kind of man that gets things done and makes no excuses along the way! *The Passage* is a book that inspires greatness in the reader. Each chapter challenges you to take a deeper look at your life to manifest the person you were meant to be!…This book will change your life!"

—Rev. Terrence E. Trimuel

"T. Dwayne's book *The Passage* has impacted the life of my daughter and countless other young people. The book helps you to focus and discover vision for your life despite life challenges. I highly recommend this book to inspire youth to become tomorrow's leaders and hone something that is as valuable as education itself—vision."

—Cynthia Sipp

The Passage

Navigating Pitfalls on Your Journey to Success

T. Dwayne Smith, LPC, NCC

The Passage: Navigating Pitfalls on Your Journey to Success

Second Edition

Copyright © 2024, T. Dwayne Smith, LPC, NCC

All rights reserved under International Copyright Law.

Contents and/or cover may not be reproduced in whole or in part in any form without the express written consent of the author except in cases of review as permitted by law.

Scripture quotations marked (NIV) are taken from the Holy Bible, New International Version®, NIV®. Copyright © 1973, 1978, 1984, 2011 by Biblica, Inc.™ Used by permission of Zondervan. All rights reserved worldwide. www.zondervan.comThe "NIV" and "New International Version" are trademarks registered in the United States Patent and Trademark Office by Biblica, Inc.™

Scripture taken from the New King James Version®. Copyright © 1982 by Thomas Nelson. Used by permission. All rights reserved.

Scriptural references marked (WEB) are taken from the World English Bible. Used by permission. WorldEnglish.Bible.

All photographs are open source distributed under a CC-BY 2.0 license.

Other images used by license or permission from the copyright holder.

Editing performed by White Arrow Press LLC.

Printed in the United States of America.

ISBN: 978-0-9908109-5-7

Permission requests may be directed to:

Team Unstoppable, Inc.
444 East Roosevelt Road, Suite #254, Lombard, IL 60148
(708) 218-1104

TeamUnstoppable.org

TDwayne01@gmail.com

Table of Contents

Dedication -- i

Special Thank You -- iii

Foreword -- v

Introduction --- vii

Chapter 1: My Passage --- 1

Chapter 2: The Enemy of Excellence Is Average --------------- 47

Chapter 3: Personal Image --- 73

Chapter 4: Attitude, the Key to Success ---------------------- 95

Chapter 5: Putting the Picture Together
        (The Power of Finished Work) ---------------------- 121

Chapter 6: Pressing Toward the Goal (Vision) -------------- 141

Salvation --- 165

Prayer of Salvation -- 167

Endnotes -- 169

About the Author --- 175

Dedication

I dedicate this book to my wife, Tannita Smith, who is my greatest cheerleader and supporter. Thank you for believing in me and encouraging me along the journey.

I also dedicate this book to my brother John and my two sisters, Delores and Jeanine. My family has been a rock in my life. Thank you all for standing by me and always encouraging me to be my very best!

To Aunt Malinda and Uncle Frank: Thank you for being there for me during some very difficult times in my life. You were very instrumental in my growth and development at a very critical time in my life. You opened up your home and your hearts and called me son after the death of my parents. Because of your support, I went from being an average student to graduating in the top 5 percent of my high school senior class. You taught me manhood, personal responsibility, hard work, endurance, and commitment. I am who I am today as a result of these life skills you taught me, and I still use the very same skills in my adult life. Love you both forever! Rest in peace, Uncle Frank and Aunt Malinda.

Finally, I dedicate this book to all the individuals who were told one time or another that "you can't," "you won't," or "you never will" achieve any success, accomplish any goals, or amount to anything or anybody in life. What I say to you is this: The formula for your success is locked inside of you. You are loaded with creative power and untapped potential. Your talent and unique abilities are unmatched by anyone else. Believe in yourself, and never, never, NEVER quit on yourself or your dreams. You have a personal responsibility to yourself to become the success you dream. Your PROCESS is necessary and essential, because it qualifies you to experience the success that you were born to become.

Special Thank You

To Mr. Coleman, a teacher at J. Sterling Morton Middle School:

Let me first start by saying, I thank God for teachers! Everyone in life, no matter where he or she is professionally, has been impacted by a teacher in some way, shape, or form. Every nurse, doctor, lawyer, politician, mechanic, actor, musician, and educator was first impacted by a teacher. A teacher has the ability to crush the dreams of a student or inspire a student to change the world for the better. I thank God that my teachers were all inspirations, especially my middle school teacher.

Mr. Coleman, I want to thank you from the bottom of my heart. Meeting you in middle school was divinely orchestrated by God Himself! My encounter with you was timely and just what I needed for that very important developmental stage of my life. You would not allow me to fail or accept failure as an option. You placed a demand on my potential, and you did not allow me to give anything less than my very best effort with my work output! I will never forget how much you cared about each and every student in your classroom. You met us where we were, and you facilitated an environment that allowed each student to maximize their individual experiences and meet with personal success. After encountering you, I realized how important my life was and that I had a say in what happened in my life. I no longer felt like a victim of circumstance, and I knew from that moment forward: NO MORE EXCUSES! Your impact on my life, launched me on a quest to positively impact every person—young and old—from that moment forward with the same simple formula: love, affirm, support, confront, and demand effort! My attitude and outlook on life is better because of your impact.

You are an example of that old saying: "It takes a village to raise a child." You were a leader in my village, and I am thankful that God placed a strong, positive, black man in my life at that critical and crucial developmental stage of my life. I was going through a lot with the loss of my mother and the ongoing struggles of being young, black, and male on the West Side of Chicago. You were the Moses sent to bring deliverance into the young, black boys and girls in your classroom. I want to take this moment to say thank you for accepting the teaching assignment at J. Sterling Morton Middle School. Your decision to work at Morton was the difference-maker in my life.

Foreword

Many people admire others from afar; their grit, their determination, their status, their success. They then have thoughts and make statements like, "I would like to be just like them one day!"

Unfortunately for those who fall into that category they have neither the tools nor an accurate appreciation of what it takes to actually get there. Chronically successful people are not who they are and have not gotten to where they are by sheer luck, happenstance, or a few random circumstances that just so happened to have gone their way. The thing many high achievers have in common is they have the ability to see where they want to be and then they have a plan—a process, if you will—in order to see their vision and goals come to fruition. T. Dwayne Smith's book *The Passage* examines and reveals best practices that will help readers equip themselves with tools and principles to take their businesses, schools, companies, and relationships from their current reality to their desired outcome.

T. Dwayne Smith is a portrait of determination, a man who has had to experience pain in order to achieve prominence. Yet he makes no excuses for himself or for any of us as to why we cannot all be a success in whatever sphere of influence that we may find ourselves in. Ever since we first met back in my freshman year at Eastern Illinois University I have found Dwayne to be one of the most driven, focused, natural leaders that I have ever met. Over twenty-five years later, he remains a consistent, committed force in the marketplace. Author, speaker, and founder and CEO of his non-profit organization Teen-Train, Inc., Dwayne is cementing his leadership legacy by ensuring that the next generation of young leaders take their rightful places in society.

The Passage will inspire you. It will challenge you. It will call you to action. Do you truly desire to grow, to excel, to take your life—both personally and professionally—to the next level? T. Dwayne Smith's book *The Passage* is a tool that will help you take the next step toward your own personal destiny.

Ray McElroy

Former Chicago Bears Team chaplain, six-year NFL player, corporate motivational speaker, and founder of A Ray of Hope on Earth
www.ARayOfHopeOnEarth.org

Introduction

If You Don't Make the Choice, the Choice Will Make You

There are provisions in place for each and every person to experience an abundantly good life. There will also be situations of hardship and issues to overcome, no matter who you are. And while anyone can find it easy to respond well when things are going well, your response to the rough times is what really counts. When disappointments, obstacles, challenges, and setbacks knock at your door…how will you respond?

Life is full of surprises and filled with challenges and inevitable changes. Something that I have come to understand through my personal journey is that life is, essentially, composed of the choices that we make and how we respond to the outcomes of our choices.

Will you choose to quit, or will you choose to keep going and preserve through the hardships?

Will you choose to throw in the towel, or will you answer the bell for one more round and keep fighting the tough times?

Will you choose to complain about how bad your situation has become, or will you choose to exercise self-control and focus on what you can learn and how you can grow through the situation?

Will you choose to settle for whatever outcomes you have, or will you choose to create the outcomes you desire in life?

Will you choose to focus on the problem, or will you readjust your lens (your thought process regarding your circumstances) and see the problem as an opportunity to grow and become a better person?

As a youngster, I remember some of the wisdom nuggets that I heard that helped to keep me focused when facing difficult challenges. One of those was, "If life gives you lemons, add some sugar and water, and you will have lemonade. Drink it, and keep moving!" During my teenage and young adult years, I was told that "success and failure share the same mindset—commitment." The central theme in both of the sayings is that the choice is clearly yours to make.

You Have the Power to Choose

In life, you will fail and make mistakes.

In some cases, people just continue in this vicious cycle of repeating the same failures and making the same mistakes—over and over again. The point that I want to impress upon you is that you have the power to choose and the ability to contribute to the future that you want for your life. My hope for everyone that reads this book is that you will slow down; be patient, count the cost, seek instruction, and take heed to the wisdom given before making major life decisions.

Your life is special and your time is valuable. Therefore, when you make important decisions, stay committed to the process, put forth your best effort, work hard, and walk in integrity. Seize every opportunity to grow and learn as an individual. One of my favorite quotes, which originated with computer scientist Alan Kay, is, "The best way to predict the future is to create it."[1]

This quote resonates with me personally because it takes away all excuses for not experiencing the life that we dream about. In essence, it speaks to a reality that we have the power and the ability to manifest our dreams. So, don't complain about what you have or don't have. Instead, create what you dream and desire for your future. You have the power and the ability to create the life that you want!

I once heard someone say, "Life is a cruel teacher. She will give you the test first and the answers later." In my opinion, while there might be some truth in the idea of life offering this method as a teaching tool, it is the worst way to learn, because the end result could come at the cost of unnecessary loss of both precious time and valuable resources. In other words, there are better ways to find out helpful or needed information than just thoughtlessly or recklessly stumbling through situations. I highly recommend that you take a contrary approach to the mindset of "experience will be your teacher" and instead become proactive, intentional, strategic, and passionate about your future. Take time to think about what you want to accomplish in your academic and professional life. Take time to dream about what you can become. Take time to think about your associations and who you are spending your time with. One of my college mentors told me, "Dwayne, if you show me your friends, I can tell you what your future will be." This simple statement had a profound impact on me, because it made me think about the power of associations.

Now, in the aim of living out "best practices," don't be afraid to make mistakes, because mistakes are a part of the learning process. No athlete became great by worrying about perfection. They took their progress one step at a time, mistakes and all, until they arrived at excellence. In my opinion, Michael Jordan's approach to greatness and the attitude that he developed about failing along the way is best articulated in the "Failure" commercial by Nike; in it, Jordan shares how he learned success, "I've missed more than 9,000 shots in my career. I've lost almost 300 games. Twenty-six times I've been trusted to take the game-winning shot and missed. I've failed over, and over, and over again in my life, and that is why I succeed."[2]

Jordan understood that in order to succeed a person must learn from failure. The key to success is failure and not being afraid to make mistakes. Failure and mistakes can help people grow and mature, if they are willing to learn and move forward as a result of the knowledge acquired from those experiences.

What Is Success?

When we talk about the topic of success, what do I mean by that idea? A lot of things may come to your mind as the answer to that question, but let me first start by sharing what success is not:

- Success is not a straight line.
- Success is not luck.

- Success is not easy.
- Success is not for the undisciplined and weak at heart.
- Success is not a shortcut in life.
- Success is not overnight.

Speaking of success and what it looks like, we are not to compare ourselves to others and measure our accomplishments against someone else's accomplishments. We should instead focus on the dreams and desires within our heart and allow the passion for these things to push us into that place of personal success and fulfillment. We sometimes think that success is predicated on wealth, job status, relationships, or material gain. The truth of the matter is, success has nothing to do with any of these things. Now, don't misunderstand what I'm saying, because obtaining these things are all byproducts of some form of success. But they alone don't equate success. In order to obtain true success, we must understand that success is a daily commitment to fulfilling our dreams through hard work, dedication, perseverance, patience, and selflessness as we endeavor to discover our God-given potential without comparing our authentic self or comparing what you've done to what you were purposed to do.

Success is a journey of self-discovery and growth that is often faced with many challenges and a lot of adversity along the way. In your pursuit of success, you will experience highs, lows, circles, and squiggles, because there is no straight-line pathway to success. In my life, most of the success that I've obtained came outside of my plans or my desired ways to achieve success. I soon realized that it was not my ability alone that opened doors and presented the life-changing opportunities before me. God's hand was on my life, and He was divinely ordering my steps along my passage, helping me to accomplish my academic and professional goals. My most valuable takeaways from my journey was learning to trust the process and embrace the product that I was becoming.

On your passage to success, you must not lose hope or grow weary because the journey is one of endurance, patience, and persistence. There is another quote (attributed to Winston Churchill) that I find helpful in unpacking this concept, and it goes like this, "Success is going from failure to failure without losing your enthusiasm."[3] In essence, failure is a part of the journey to succeed in life. The key is to never give up while going through the process to become successful; because if you give up and quit, you will neither achieve nor experience true success. We all have God-given dreams, goals, and aspirations. The good news is this: God has already equipped you and me with everything that we need to be successful in life.

Never give up on your dreams!
Never give up on yourself!
Never give up on God!

Your SUCCESS is on the inside. It is your responsibility to work it from the inside out.

Chapter 1

My Passage

"Give me six hours to chop down a tree, and I will spend the first four sharpening the axe."

—Abraham Lincoln[4]

Think about Lincoln's quote for a minute: "Give me six hours to chop down a tree, and I will spend the first four sharpening the axe."[4] What do you think this quote is saying? I believe this quote is speaking directly to the process of preparation! President Lincoln understood that preparation was key to seizing current and new opportunities. Too often, we neglect the "process" of preparation because we are focused on the "product," which is the result of the preparation. The *American Dictionary of the English Language* defines the word *process* as:

> A proceeding or moving forward; progressive course; tendency; as the *process* of man's desire. Course; continual flux or passage; as the *process* of time.[5]

I am sure that most of you have heard the following statements...

- "For every action there is an equal but opposite reaction."
- "For every start there is a finish."
- "To everything there is a season."
- "What you sow, you will reap."

I'd also like for you to become familiar with my saying: "The process equals the product!"

The quotes can go on and on and on. The point that I want to make is this: Nothing "just happens"! *Everything* is a process or a form of preparation that ultimately leads to a final product.

Everything in life operates by way of a process. The process or preparation you invest into something will determine the product or end result that you will have. If you had a master chef prepare an original dish one hundred times, that chef would use the same process or procedure of operation every time to arrive at the same desired result or product. The chef uses the same step-by-step process to ensure that the product would successfully and systematically manifest time after time after time.

Preparing for your future is the process. The product will be the end result of that preparation. If your product is undesirable, modify your process or preparation. It's that simple! As you can see from the quote by Lincoln, the most important part of chopping down the tree was the preparation of the cutting tool itself—before a person would begin the physical process of cutting down the tree.

I was at a business conference some years ago. I heard one of the speakers make this simple, yet profound statement: "If you want something different, you have to be willing to do something different." In other words, you will not experience change until *you* see the need for change and understand that change is often not true change until *you* change. You have to make the commitment to change. You have to be willing to change your process in order to experience a different product or end result.

The Passage Begins

When you read the word *passage*, what comes to your mind? There could be a lot of different images or ideas of what represents a passage. But one thing is shared by most, if not all, of those things: A passage involves a journey. It involves moving from one point to another, often through a space that involves shadows, challenges, or simply the unknown. And, just as often, it leads to something better or more desirable than where the journey-taker started.

With this in mind, I would like to share the early parts of my "passage" (life process) with you. My hope is that my personal experiences will ignite something inside you that will compel you to do something different in order to experience something different. The process is continual and subject to change, with or without your approval (and oftentimes without notification).

April Fool's Day

At the age of nine years old, I remember having this horrible dream that seemed so real. I could literally feel the tears streaming down the side of my face as I was asleep, or so I thought.

All of a sudden, I heard two voices, both calling my name, "Dwayne, get up! Get up, Dwayne! Dwayne—get up!" I quickly realized that the voices were those of my grandmother and my aunt, attempting to wake up my older brother and me. They needed to inform us that our mother had passed away while in the hospital.

I was between a state of sleep and consciousness and thinking to myself, "Am I dreaming, or is this now my reality? Oh, God, let it be anything but true!" I soon realized that my worst nightmare was now my devastating reality.

As my grandmother and aunt shared the nature of my mother's death, my brother and I wept and embraced each other. The sadness was so overwhelming and the pain of the loss was so deep that I wanted to be with my mother in death at that very moment.

The mere thought of living life without my mother was unbearable. While driving home afterward with my father and two sisters, we were all quiet and processing the reality that we all now had to face. I had looked to my mom for strength, hope, joy, confidence, and faith. Who would fill her shoes now, and how could I make it without her? I had to learn at a tender young age that this was only a part of my process of becoming the man who I am today.

As I traveled home from my grandmother's house, I remained in disbelief. My state of mind was one of complete denial! It was unbelievable how my life had changed overnight. This was no April Fool's joke, even though my mother died on the first of April. I began to ponder the following questions:

- "How are we going to make it as a family?"
- "Why did my mother have to die?"
- "What am I going to do without my mother?"

They were questions that even adults ponder after the loss of a close loved one.

While the grief cycle was taking its course, I became overwhelmed, all at once. I was confused; full of fear, frustration, disbelief, and hopelessness. Life without my mother was something that I could not or would not imagine.

Can you fathom being a child who is growing up motherless? Well, this was now my situation, and this process was not an easy one. To be honest, I had no indication that this terrible circumstance would be the building blocks in my life to become the person I am today. The Bible says, "You intended to harm me, but God intended it for good to accomplish what is now being done, the saving of many lives" (Gen. 50:20 NIV).

Coping

As my father began to comfort us and offer what little support he could, I could clearly see that he was not coping well with the loss of his beloved wife. I witnessed my father's motivation, desire, and will to live diminish with each passing day. My father had already been what you would call a "functioning alcoholic." He was very high functioning, but his outlet or vice was alcohol. He would literally get up everyday, have a cup of coffee, look over bills, leave for work, come home, get us dinner, and then drink until he fell asleep. After the death of my mother, though, his drinking progressively worsened to the point that his daily functionality became impaired. I did not realize it at the time, but now, as a therapist, I understand that my father was struggling with the emotional process of grieving the loss of his wife, and that while making major life adjustments without any emotional support as a single parent of four children, including being the sole provider. My father suppressed his feelings and tried to do the best he could, to his own detriment.

Hope Deferred

I hoped and prayed that my father would turn his life around, stop drinking, and take better care of himself—if not for himself, then for the sake of his children. However, it seemed like nothing was getting better, only growing worse. The passing of my mother triggered a downward spiral in my father's life that was due primarily to a lack of knowledge, understanding, emotional support, and professional counseling services that could help to address the grief and loss that we were all experiencing in our own individual ways.

As a result of my father's condition worsening, with us children being in the home alone often (without any parental supervision), neighbors and family members became concerned for our safety. Eventually, someone anonymously notified the Department of Children and Family Services (DCFS) to address the issues and concerns. Despite all of the confusion and dysfunction that arose out of the DCFS investigation, somehow—someway—we remained together as a family unit. This battle was won, but the war was far from over!

As time went on, I became increasingly bitter and angry about my life situation. I had a victim mentality that was being cultivated daily. I internalized the hurt and disappointments and developed severe abandonment and trust issues. I didn't understand it at that time, but what I perceived as anger was actually hurt. Anger is a secondary emotion. The primary emotion that I was struggling with was deep emotional hurt, and because I didn't understand emotional regulation, I lacked the ability and appropriate coping skills to exert control over my emotional state. Therefore, I struggled with anxiety, fear, sadness, and overwhelming thoughts of failure in life. The only emotion I felt gave me some sense of power was anger and lashing out at others. You know the saying, "hurt people hurt people." After the passing of my mother, everything seemed so difficult and challenging. This was pressure that I neither knew before, nor did I have the skills to handle. My focus was now just surviving from day to day.

Every account of my life's circumstances that I have relayed until now indicates that I was becoming a product of my environment. My environment became one of turbulence, uncertainty, fear, and frustration. Many youth and families in today's society can identify with these feelings. My environmental conditions were shaping my attitude, outlook, mindset, and, finally, my behavior.

Environmental Conditions Influence Behavior

Stephen Covey once said, "Reactive people…are often affected by their physical environment. They find external sources to blame for their behavior."[6]

I was reactive as a result of my environment. I found myself in fight-or-flight mode daily, because I didn't know whom I could trust since the people who were closest to me were the ones who had disappointed and hurt me the most. Environmental conditions were extreme, and they had adverse affects on my mindset, mentality, and attitude about life and people in general. When I think about the power and impact that environment has on behavior, the best illustration that I've heard that captures the meaning of this point is the story I once heard about the piranha and the goldfish.

Someone told me about an experiment where a piranha and goldfish were used to prove the theory that environmental factors, either controlled or uncontrolled, can shape, influence, and determine behaviors and outcomes. In the experiment, a red-bellied piranha was placed in a fish tank with a goldfish, and the red-bellied piranhas are the most aggressive of the twenty different species of piranha.

The piranha's natural instincts kicked in, and it began to spread out in search of prey; on the other hand, the goldfish's natural instinct is to seek out shelter and safety when danger is present. To prove the hypothesis that environment influences behavior, a glass plate was inserted in the middle of the fish tank, to create a divide between the goldfish and the piranha. After a while, the goldfish came out of hiding, and the piranha made eye contact. Once the piranha saw the goldfish, it went on an aggressive attack to subdue it. The piranha was met with resistance as it hit its head up against the glass window, fruitlessly trying to devour the goldfish. This behavior continued over a period of time, and the frequency of the piranha's attempts to get the goldfish decreased day by day.

After a week or so, the piranha had become extremely passive and withdrawn. Finally, the glass window was removed from the tank, and both the goldfish and the piranha could swim around the entirety of it. The goldfish immediately started to freely swim about, because it no longer sensed danger in the waters—it even brushed up against the now-dying and paralyzed piranha.

Eventually, the piranha died from starvation, because the environmental conditions had been set and a mental block had developed that told the piranha that it could not have access to its natural prey. The experiment proved that once the environmental conditions are set, then attitudes, mindsets, mentalities, and behaviors can come under the influence of the factors of the environment.

The piranha lost its potential and ability to pursue and devour the goldfish without struggle to a mindset of despondency, inadequacy and hopelessness. The experiment makes me think about the people from my childhood who helped to foster this same "can't win in life" and "success is not for everyone" mindset. Just like the piranha, you can see the opportunities, however, due to your environmental conditions that are set and reinforced by observation, association, and (wrong) teaching, you adopt the mindset that you can't have it, and you settle for status quo in life…or worse!

We were all born with individual, unique gifts and talents that set us all apart. We all have giftedness that is unmatched! However, just like the glass window that was intentionally placed in the fish tank to prevent the piranha from maximizing his potential, situations and circumstances can set up a mindset with unhelpful mental walls, barriers, and obstacles, establishing environmental conditions that foster and reinforce a mindset of hopelessness, defeat, fear, and despair. As a result, you embrace the attitude of "I can't, so why try?"

I've lost count of the number of people—both young and old—who lived by this mindset. Like the programmed mind of the piranha, you can see and hear about all the resources that are available to help you pursue your hopes and dreams…but these outside options are no good to you until the *inside* options are rightly chosen. The root issue behind the "mental block" can also create a "behavioral block" that needs to be removed as well.

Let's go back to the quote by Steven Covey, "Reactive people…find external sources to blame for their behavior."[6] This sort of "reaction" that Covey refers to became my go-to, because I started to blame external sources for my outward behaviors and used every excuse for not experiencing success in life. I started to blame external resources from my environment that said:

- You are not good enough.
- You can't do it.

- You don't have the skills.
- No one else around you has done it.
- It will not work!

You can dream of greatness, but if your environment does not cultivate nor does it support the dream to be great, then, usually, the end result is the same as the piranha. Those results tend to be:

1. Starvation
2. Stagnation
3. Death

What do you think would have happened if Michael Jordan; Dr. Charles Drew; Fredrick Douglass; Martin Luther King, Jr.; Booker T. Washington; George Washington Carver; or even my pastor, Dr. Bill Winston (to borrow an example from more modern times), had allowed the glass walls of their environments to stop them from pursuing their dreams? You don't have to answer—I'll simply tell you: We would not know their stories! We would not know their names! They would not be a part of American history for their accomplishments, because they would not have stepped beyond the walls of containment to pursue their dreams!

Environment is so important—it sets the atmosphere for your potential to come forth. Again, the piranha *naturally* had the potential to pursue, overtake, and devour the goldfish. However, the environmental conditions that were set—by a temporary glass window—first limited the piranha's perception, which then restricted its potential, which next created a mindset of self-containment, which finally reinforced a sense of limitation.

What is in your environment that might be stifling, containing, and limiting your potential? Honestly ask yourself:

- Is there a fear of failure (or even fear of success)?
- Is there a shame from your past?
- Is there a trauma from your childhood?
- Is there a lack of faith?
- Is there a lack of motivation?
- Are there negative people in your life?
- Is there a lack of knowledge?

If there is something, don't let starvation, stagnation, and death steal your hopes and dreams.

If you have a dream, trust the process, because doing so will place you in the perfect situation for your dream to become your reality. There is value and importance in the right environment. Sometimes, the right environment is not the most comfortable place; however, it's ideal for cultivating your gift and working your potential from the inside out.

On the negative end, if you stay contained and in the wrong environment, your potential and creative ability will become stifled; frustration will start to build, forward progress will be compromised, and you will inevitably forfeit your purpose, which is tied to the reason for your very existence.

You have to make the commitment to being successful, even if your current situation doesn't look the way that you want it to right now. If you are committed, even if your current environment or conditions seem counterproductive to what you desire, you will at some point see circumstances start to shift, and your environment or conditions will begin to place a demand on your potential. Eventually, greatness will become your outcome.

Your circumstances cannot keep you from the direction that you need to go as long as you're committed to getting there. It might take longer, but heading in the right direction still counts in the end. In other words, your mindset and outlook on life will change your mental environment, which will change your perceptions, which will change your potential. Some people call this the law of attraction.

Take, for example, the story of the Jewish patriarch Joseph. According to the Bible, in Genesis 37, God gave Joseph a dream that would combat a coming global economic crisis. When Joseph shared his dreams of ruling and reigning, his family did not embrace his dream. In fact, they despised him for sharing his dreams. After hearing Joseph's dreams, his family thought Joseph had a superiority complex over them and they despised him for it. Joseph's environment became one of tension, stress, turmoil, and sorrow—all the "right" elements to kill a dream! However, God intervened on Joseph's behalf and—through the course of many years and a trying series of events—placed Joseph in the right environment for his gifts to be embraced, encouraged, and sought after. By going through the process, by refusing to let different barriers define his destiny, Joseph became what he dreamed: A ruler, a leader, and the answer for the world crisis in his time. Joseph's dream eventually became his reality (see Gen. 42).

Don't let your environment kill your dreams! Unlike that piranha, you don't have to die with your potential locked inside. Just like a seed requires the proper environment (light, soil, and moisture) and thrives upon being surrounded with what's needed, your right environment will help catapult you and place you on the trajectory of success.

Sticks and Stones

Remember the age old adage: "Sticks and stones may break my bones, but words will never hurt me!"

If you were told all your life that "You will never amount to anything," or "You are not good enough," or "You have no value or worth to anybody or anything," how do you think these negative deposits will impact your self-esteem, self-image, and decision-making? Take a moment and reflect on this.

If you allow these negative words to linger and swim around in your mind, the effects of these words will eventually set up boundaries in your heart and potentially shift you away from your purpose.

The Bible says in Proverbs 23:7 (WEB), "For as he thinks about the cost, so he is. 'Eat and drink!' he says to you, but his heart is not with you." This is a very powerful truth, because it implies that if you can think and believe a certain way in your heart (yes, you can THINK with your heart), it will be powerful enough to govern future words, actions, habits, character. Eventually, our thoughts can impact our ultimate destiny in life.

Let's look at it from a positive perspective. Consider what would happen if a person is consistently told:

- You are smart.
- You are a winner.
- You can make a difference.
- If you can dream it, you can achieve it.

The same spiritual law pointed out in that proverb goes into action. The force of the words above will eventually build in someone's heart and mind the image of courage, assurance, and confidence that will propel him or her on the path of success in life. So, I would like to say it this way, "Sticks and stones may break your bones, but words will determine your future!" What goes in, must come out. It's a law!

As a youngster, negative words were spoken *to me, about me,* and *in my environment* on a daily basis. As a consequence, until I understood how to take ownership of my outcomes, my actions began to align with the words that were spoken in my atmosphere.

Words are so powerful! They are invisible and, until spoken or expressed (inwardly or outwardly), inert. However, once released into the atmosphere of our lives, these same invisible and inert words become a powerful force that has the potential to shift the atmosphere and influence attitudes, mindsets, behaviors, and outcomes.

A great example of this reality is demonstrated in an approximately twenty-three minute video by Rocky Kanaka. His video is about changing the perception, the approachability, and, finally, the relational ability of a dog in the pound. The dog, still considered young at only three years old, had been named Venom by her previous owners. During the video, Rocky changes the dog's name to Honey, and he treats her as a sweet animal rather than a vicious one. The dog that begins the interaction with a growl seems like a completely different animal by the time that the video concludes.[7]

My environment was one that fostered negativity, fear, and defeat as a result of the words that were spoken. If you pour coffee out of a pot and into a cup, the contents don't change. The color, flavor, and temperature remain the same as it transfers from one container into another. Just because the coffee was taken from one location and placed in another doesn't change the fact that what was in the pot is the same thing in the cup—coffee.

The same concept holds true if your environment is one that fosters fear, unbelief, doubt, or negativity. The people who grew up in these toxic environments can change their geographical location, but—just like the coffee that was once in the pot and then transferred to a cup—the same distorted attitude, mindset, and behaviors will eventually manifest in that new environment. I'm sure you've heard the saying that "you can take the person out of the ghetto, but you can't take the ghetto out of the person."

My point is this: Who you are today is a direct result of where you've been and what you've experienced in your life. My environment was plagued with dysfunction, so I exhibited a mindset and behaviors that were dysfunctional in nature. Did this progression in a negative direction mean the end of my potential? No. It did mean that I had things to now work through though, things that, had my environment been more positive, I might have walked through to a far lesser degree (if at all) during that phase of my development.

Now, imagine a dysfunctional person operating in the capacity of an educator, therapist, parent, clergy, elected government official, influential community member, or business leader. When someone in a negative state is also in a state of influence or power, it leads to a perpetual cycle of hurting people who are now hurting other people (or at least have a high potential to do so)! No matter how we choose to articulate the concept, it all boils down to the same well-known fact: "Garbage in equals garbage out!"

Every seed must and will produce after its own kind—it's a law!

Failure and Success Both Require Energy

The effort and energy that is required to achieve or overcome when facing difficult times or challenges in life is also required to *under*achieve or remain a victim to your circumstance. I had an attitude of "I don't care," and it required a lot of effort and energy to maintain that posture.

When offered help, I would refuse it. When given opportunities, I would simply pass on them. My behavior was an outward expression of emotional hurt, rejection, dejection, and lack of self-worth. What I found to be interesting was that my environment was influencing and encouraging this dysfunctional mindset that had me on autopilot, leading me to reject opportunities and turn down much-needed support and assistance. I was aware, at times; but most of the time, I was unaware of how my mindset manifested into my actions. My entire family shared this mindset, at times. We all had serious trust issues, and we all refused to allow anyone to get emotionally close to us. We all walked around, in silence, while going through deep, emotional storms. In the years following the death of our parents, I never received professional help to deal with my grief. Therefore, I responded like most traumatized pre-teens would: I bottled up the hurt and stopped caring about anything of value. I adopted the "I don't care" attitude about my life and outwardly expressed my anger.

All It Takes Is One

Mr. Coleman, my eighth-grade teacher, for some strange reason took a special interest in me. He was my homeroom teacher, so I had him all day long.

He was very concerned about my lack of social engagement in class and my restricted range of emotion when expressing myself. Mr. Coleman began to challenge my negative thinking, defeated attitude, and self-destructive behaviors while in school. Mr. Coleman would share his educational philosophy daily and most times, he would write it on the blackboard: "Give me your best, and nothing but your best!"

It was pretty obvious to Mr. Coleman that I was not giving my best effort; therefore he continued to push, pull, and draw out my potential until he was convinced that I gave him my absolute best in class. Mr. Coleman made a lasting impression on my life through his relentless efforts to tap into my potential and convince me to release it in the classroom and in life.

As a father, mentor to so many students, and professional counselor, I now understand that you have to be intentional about your mission and purposeful with your actions if you want to invoke change in the lives of others. Mr. Coleman recognized my state of mind, and he slowly and consistently moved me out of a mindset of failure, defeat, despair, and rejection, calling me up into a mindset that embraced self-efficacy, confidence, personal accountability, and success.

Mr. Coleman helped me to understand what potential was, how to tap into my potential, and, more importantly, that failure and success both required the same commitment and mindset to manifest. He helped me to understand the value of Winston Churchill's words when the former prime minister had made this very powerful and profound statement, "Success is not final, failure is not fatal: it is the courage to continue that counts."[8]

I began to understand that the life that I live from this day forward will be the direct result of the choices that I make (both good and bad) from this day forward. I began to understand through the love and concern of my teacher that my life mattered!

It's interesting how your environment will not only tell you who you are; your environment will tell you what you *can* and *cannot* do, where you *can* and *cannot* go, and who you *can* and *cannot* become.

Mr. Coleman helped me to see that the victim mindset that I had was the reason that I couldn't see myself learning, growing, or becoming anything different that how I had thought of myself up to a certain point in life. It took someone from the outside to be daring and loving enough to come inside my chaotic world and effect change for the better—change that was mainly instigated by his words applied to my life.

The experience of his ground-breaking instruction helped me to not only begin to see but also to understand that whatever I become in life is a direct product of my willingness or unwillingness to accept responsibility for my actions. I learned that I had to tap into my hidden abilities or "potential," so that I could begin to release my inner greatness, so that others would be inspired to move beyond the limitations of their thoughts. Mr. Coleman created a classroom environment that was both safe and conducive to learning. His daily message to his classroom was this, "You are special, unique—and you will make a positive contribution to this world!" Mr. Coleman's efforts sparked passion, purpose, desire, and a thirst for success within me, and I am so thankful to this very day.

To every teacher and parent who reads my book, please grasp this concept and run with it. Your children or students can change, learn, and achieve success. Every person is born with purpose and potential. Begin to resist what is familiar just because "that's the way it's always been," and instead embrace what *can be* in the life of your child or student.

In the midst of encouraging you to encourage yourself and others, let me say that I once heard someone say, "I don't care what you know until I know that you care." This statement is a game changer! Just think for a moment, if we as parents, leaders, and educators could set aside our ego and intellect for a moment and simply start to *care* about the life and person of the student or child (or whoever else we may have influence in the life of), that individual will know that you care and start to care about what you know. This is called *relationship*! Mr. Coleman would make time to listen, observe, validate feelings, show genuine love and support, encourage, and hold accountable. And guess what? All the students in our class respected him, and we worked as hard as we could to impress him and show him that we cared just as much as he cared about our education.

Demand Success and Nothing Less from Yourself

Your children or students or employees will rise to the standard that you set for them, whether low or high. I speak from personal experience.

Mr. Coleman placed a demand on my potential, and he remained consistent with his expectations. I then rose to the expectations that he had set for me. Until Mr. Coleman, no one had demanded anything more from me than what I was already doing. Since there was no standard or expectation for me to strive for beyond what I was already experiencing in life, there was also no sense of challenge or a desire to do anything differently.

The only expectation that you should have for yourself is SUCCESS! Always remember that success is personal! As a professional school counselor, licensed professional counselor, and father, I have three basic expectations of those in my care or under my tutelage:

- Take personal accountability for your actions.
- Be consistent in your efforts to accomplish your personal and professional goals.
- Expect growth in your life and embrace the change that you desire.

A Change for the Better

As a result of Mr. Coleman's positive attitude, affirming words, high academic expectations, and the win-win culture that he established with his students, my life began to change for the better. My attitude changed, and I developed self-efficacy in my own ability to succeed at a task or goal that I was faced with. I made the honor roll for the first time in my life, and it felt so good to finally get attention for doing something that was *positive*. This was something totally new for me, and—for the first time—I did not feel helpless, hopeless, and powerless. I instead felt that I had the power to change the outcome of my life through my own efforts, attitude, and consistent commitment to doing what was required to be successful.

When they say that one person can make a difference, I am living proof of that statement. As a result of one person taking the time to show genuine concern and demanding next-level effort for success, my life changed for the better. The fact that this one teacher took the time to say things such as "You will succeed in my class," in turn, fostered a mindset of personal value, self-worth, and intrinsic motivation.

Leaving the Past Behind

I was motivated, and I was soaring in school. My attendance, attitude, and grades had completely turned around. Going to school was no longer something that I dreaded. I looked forward to getting to school on time and learning something new every day. I took personal responsibility and great pride in becoming one of the most-improved students in the eighth grade.

I was excited about going to high school, because I felt like I was ready for the academic challenge of high school and like I had the confidence to compete at the next level of my academics. The community where I had grown up was ridden with gang violence, drugs, and poverty. My dad was now drinking less, and he became concerned with the ongoing crime and violence in our community, so he surprised us all by purchasing a home, moving us away from the influences of our old community.

The move could not have come at a better time. We were so proud and happy about the decision that our father made to finally move, because we were seeing things change for the worse all around us. The future was looking better and brighter just through that transition to a healthier, more hopeful location. I went from a kid who didn't care about anything (including my future) to being a freshman at John Marshall Metro High School and soaring academically.

Doors were starting to fly open, and it seemed as if people were "on assignment" to encourage me. I recall the first day of high school—my division teacher made a very profound statement that helped me to remain focused on winning in life. She said, "Today is the first day of your new beginning." This very simple statement sent chills throughout my body, because I knew that very moment, my life would never be the same! I felt supported by my family, and I had acquired two amazing friends who are still my friends to this very day, O'brien Jenkins and Eric Walker. A third friend, Derrick Jones, was also in the picture at this time; unfortunately, he would tragically pass away, though I remain grateful for our time of friendship. I also had wonderful teachers in high school—people who continued what Mr. Coleman had started, challenging me academically to put forth my very best.

All the talk about success finally convinced me that I *could* be successful. Experiencing success was still new territory for me, and it continued to require a paradigm shift. For so long, all I had thought about was failing and wasting my life away. Because of my childhood trauma, I had become pessimistic, guarded, scared, nervous, and unwilling to trust anyone. But as a result of the positive experiences that I was now having, the realization that LIFE IS CHOICE DRIVEN became my reality, and I made the choice to put in the necessary work so that I would be successful, no matter what!

Your Life Is the Sum Product of Your Choices

Over time, especially with so many dynamics of my life being beyond my control, I came to the realization that I could not control the environmental conditions. However—and please hear me on this point, because this second part is the one that I most often see people miss, which leads to them missing out in life, even when they don't have to—I *could* make decisions for my life that were *not* indicative of my environment. I didn't have control over everything, but there were some things that I could take responsibility for; and, through taking ownership, that accountability helped to influence the outcomes.

In one of his books, Martin Luther—the famous reformer who pushed back on needless traditions of his day and exhorted those around him to look to the truth of God's Word for the truth about life—recounted a dialogue between two followers of Christ: "Thereupon the old father said: Dear brother, you cannot prevent the birds from flying in the air over your head, but you can prevent them from building a nest in your hair."[9] My takeaway from those words is this: You can't stop the negative thoughts from coming; however, you can prevent the thoughts from taking up residency in your mind.[9] It's important to take control of your thoughts, because they can determine outcomes in your life.

I began to understand that I was not a victim. I had the power to refuse certain attitudes and mindsets as well as to resist the urge to act out of fear. The realization that I could take ownership over certain actions, attitudes, and behaviors helped me to understand that losing my mother at an early age and growing up with a functional alcoholic father—as tragic as those realities were—were no longer an excuse for me to keep choosing to fail in life. The dysfunctional dynamics of my homelife were no longer an automatically determining factor to me—they presented trials, but they did not get to rule over me like a tyrant. What other people thought about me did not matter more than what I thought of me (or, as I would discover later on, what the Lord thought of me). I finally realized that I had the confidence and power to choose the mindset, attitude, and life that I wanted for my future. Sometimes, the different obstacles, potholes, and challenges are out of your control and not a byproduct of your own doing. However, your attitude and response in dealing with the various circumstances and situations becomes solely your responsibility.

You have the power and ability to choose where you end up in life. So, I challenge you to stop making excuses. Stop saying, "I can't do it!" Stop being a victim of your circumstances, and don't let anybody put you in a box. You are bigger than a box of unfortunate circumstances or a rough start or unfavorable odds! Think outside the box, so that you can knock down the walls of containment that might exist in your own mind. You can make up your mind today and make "today" the first day of a new beginning in your life. Don't let your circumstances dictate your responses in life. Remember, you have the power, now choose your destiny.

All in the Master Plan

My freshman year of high school was awesome! My father would often encourage me to continue to work hard and to do my very best in school. I could see that he was proud of me and the success that I was now experiencing in my education. At the close of my first year of high school, I obtained my first job through a summer employment program, where I was mentoring and tutoring middle school students. There had been a time when I didn't care about school. Now, I was getting paid to inspire, encourage, and assist students with their academics and behavior.

I was really feeling good about the success that I was experiencing in my life. It did wonders for my self-esteem and confidence. I had a successful freshman year of high school and my first paying job. I often think about the familiar story of David and Goliath. According to the story, David had to overcome many challenges, such as slaying a lion and a bear before he had the confidence to take on the ultimate challenge—the giant Goliath! Like David, you and I must come face to face with obstacles and challenges, so that we can build character, confidence, and faith and overcome negative circumstances in life. No matter what obstacles we face as we travel this road called destiny, if we stick to the master plan, everything is going to work out for our good!

Daddy, I Need You!

While working my summer job, my relationship with my father began to take a turn for the worst. My father felt that I should use the money I earned from my summer job to pay some of the household expenses. I understood the idea of helping out my family, however, I was very disappointed at the seeming request, because school was getting ready to start and I wanted to use the small amount of money that I had made during the summer to purchase school materials, clothes, and have some extra spending money on hand during the school year.

My father became very upset with me, and I believe part of his inability to regulate his emotions was due primarily to his drinking issues. My father gave me an ultimatum: pay bills or get out! My father became so enraged about my explanation for keeping some of my money that he went into his bedroom, got his gun, and then told me to get out of his house or else he was going to kill me. I was both scared and angry. I had no income, school was getting ready to start again, and now my father was demanding me to leave the house. I could not believe this was happening. I felt rejected by my father. I could not understand his thought process or his unreasonable expectations. It appeared as soon as things were coming together in my life, they were now rapidly—and dramatically—coming apart!

I asked my father if I could call my Aunt Malinda and Uncle Frank, to see if they would come and pick me up. My dad yelled at the top of his voice, "I want you out of my house—you can go to the streets for all I care!"

My uncle, who was my father's brother, came over and attempted to calm things down. My father was adamant about his position, and he wanted me out of his house immediately. As I packed my things, I felt so deeply hurt by the words that my father had said to me. I felt rejected and all alone. This entire experience was a very difficult time for me, because I loved my dad, but I also knew that he had a very serious drinking problem. Exiting his household was a major life change for me, because I had always been with my family—it was all I had known since the death of my mother. I was overwhelmed with sadness as I hugged my brother and sisters and left the house with my Uncle Frank. As the door closed behind me, all I could do was cry, because I didn't think that I could ever forgive my father for forcing me to leave my family.

Before going further with the story, I would like to take the opportunity to express that God was faithful to provide a "means" for me in the midst of the rejection that I was walking through during this season in my life. While the heartache was heavy, my Heavenly Father—though I had yet to fully meet Him—was already living up to the promise of support that we find in Psalm 27:10 (NIV), which speaks to the reality that, even if our parents "forsake" us (see Strong's 5800, which can also be translated as "to leave" or "to loose"),[10] the Lord will take care of us. Instead of keeping me under the authority of a father who struggled with alcoholism, God allowed me to be transferred, if you will, to a place that could offer more stability and example healthier standards in that season. It wasn't what I wanted. I wouldn't even say it was necessarily what I "needed," but I would like to point out that my situation was something that God *redeemed*, in spite of how hard it was for me to walk through it.

Total Recall

My father's health continued to worsen with each passing day, until my father eventually passed away from a massive heart attack.

I can recall vividly the day that my father died. My Uncle Frank had received an emergency phone call from a mutual friend regarding the serious health issues that my father was experiencing and that time was of the essence. My uncle told me to come with him to check in on my father.

As we were rushing through the traffic to get to my father's house, I could only think about the breakdown in our relationship. During the ride, I began to reflect on my time with my father and my mother. The feelings of fear, anxiety, anger, and despair quickly began to grip my mind. My siblings were present when we arrived.

My father was sitting in the living room on the edge of the couch with a distressed look on his face. It was sad and painful to see him in this helpless condition, especially since he had always been a physically strong man. I remember sitting at his feet, encouraging him and saying that everything was going to be fine, even though I could see that he was struggling to breathe. I was scared because the situation did not look good at all. I remained at my fathers' feet, watching, waiting, and listening—hoping that he would hold on until the ambulance arrived. My father, who tried to never show signs of weakness or emotion, continued to assure us that he was okay and that all he needed was some fresh air and a glass of water.

My father and I began to reconcile and mend our differences, and a very powerful exchange of forgiveness took place. I asked my father to forgive me for my actions. I apologized for holding anger against him, and I told my father that I loved him. My father responded that he loved me and asked for my forgiveness as well. He looked me in the eyes and told me that everything was going to be okay. That exchange seemed like it took hours, yet it was a very brief moment.

The paramedics finally arrived and began to treat my father. I recall my brother and uncle bargaining with my father, trying to get him to cooperate with the medical staff. As my father attempted to stand up, he fell back into the arms of my brother. This was a painful moment, as we all felt totally helpless. The paramedics finally got my father out of the house and into the ambulance for immediate medical attention. While the paramedics were tending to our father, all we could do was stand by, reassuring each other that everything was going to be alright.

How Do I Say Goodbye—Again?

The paramedics continued their emergency procedure on my father for approximately thirty minutes before driving off to the hospital. In my head, I knew that it was over and that my father was not going to make it. However, my heart kept telling my mind to calm down and to stop thinking the worst. By this point, I had learned through my own challenges to stay in control of my thoughts and to try to think the best, no matter what. We all got into the car and followed the ambulance to the hospital only to find out upon arrival that our father had been pronounced dead. I felt so empty and numb upon receiving the news. I didn't know how to express what I was feeling in that life-changing moment, so I maintained my silence.

The adjustment after the death of my father was difficult, because he was the last stabilizing force for the family, even in his dysfunctional state. The main difference for us at this time was that, in the aftermath of the loss, my siblings and I now had to "make it happen" when it came to daily life! With both of our parents gone, we were going to have to step up to the plate to make up for the absence of such an important resource and form of relationship in our own lives.

A Work in Progress

After the funeral of my father, the trauma and feelings of loneliness were present daily. I had to fight just to get up and keep moving. I then made a decision within myself that I would not allow the legacy of my parents to be a legacy of death and brokenness. As a result, in spite of all the new challenges that I was now facing after the death of my father, I was determined to work harder than ever in school, maintain my focus, and keep a positive attitude. Part of this determination came from a realization—one which I had come across as I reflected on my situation. I had realized that I had the opportunity to eat from two different tables: The table of remaining in past failures, low self-esteem, and defeat or the table of continuing to seek success and make forward progress.

It didn't take a rocket scientist to realize which table offered the better options: the table of seeking success and making forward progress. Therefore, I remained seated and continued to "partake" of success, regardless of my personal adversities and emotional challenges. I was determined that I was not going to succumb to the negative thoughts that once plagued my mind and governed my actions. I understood that in order for me to overcome my adversity, I had to believe that success was my destiny.

Pomp and Circumstance

High school graduation was a big, big deal for me. Not only did I graduate, but I also graduated with high honors! Thanks to changes that had started back in middle school, I excelled academically, socially, and relationally during my years at John Marshall Metro High School. I remember sitting on the stage at my graduation—among other members of the National Honor Society, all of us in our white gowns—and thinking about the process and journey that had led to positive outcomes or healthy involvement in my life.

Remember the downcast, depressed middle schooler that Mr. Coleman had to challenge so much in order to get him to think beyond living in "survival mode"? Well, that young man had changed! By the grace of God, despite all the restraints that were offered in my youth, the progress that I had achieved by graduation included:

- Being part of the top 5 percent of my graduating class.
- Having membership in the National Honor Society.
- Being mentioned in *Who's Who Among American High School Students*.
- Having a role within the Principal's Scholars Program.
- Being a member of the John Hope African American Club.
- Winning the Chicago Mercantile Exchange Essay Contest Award.

- Being one of the All-City Academic Olympic History Team first-place winners.
- Being homecoming king.
- Receiving acceptance into eighteen different colleges and universities.

All of these changes and achievements went through my mind while I was sitting on that stage with the top students of my class. Although my parents were not physically present to share in this momentous occasion, I felt that they were with me in spirit. Especially when I received my high school diploma, that perceived point of contact meant everything to me, because it meant that I had accomplished my goal. There is an indescribable feeling of joy and relief that overcomes you when you finish what you started. I had finished high school well (against all odds), and I felt my parents looking down from up above, saying, "That's our boy!" Mom and Dad, this diploma is for you!

Navigating the Pitfall to Success

I was college-bound, and I was excited! I had made it out of "the 'hood'"! I remember when my Aunt Malinda dropped me off on Eastern Illinois University's campus so that I could begin my undergraduate journey. The experience of that moment was surreal. I had to take a moment and take it all in because, given my circumstance, I was a part of a population of black youth that was not supposed to "make it," according to the opinion or expectations of some. But God.

I was nervous, but my high school friends who had also decided to attend Eastern—O'brien, Derrick, and Eric—and I were determined to finish what we had all started together. I had learned the power of association through my friendships, and we valued the importance of holding each other accountable to achieve our ultimate goal (at the time)—a college degree!

Pressing Toward the Mark

In four years, I successfully graduated college and was invited to apply for a graduate assistantship within the housing department, in order to obtain my advanced degree along with gaining professional work experience as a counselor. It would be a great opportunity to provide counseling services to college students while building professional relationships. I was very excited about the potential of what could come from this opportunity to not only gain work experience but also to help people, which is something that I absolutely love to do.

Even though I didn't meet the minimum requirement of being a previous resident assistant, I still applied and interviewed for the job. To my surprise, I was offered the position. During my travel time back to campus to start my new journey, there was plenty of time and opportunity for negative thoughts to flood my mind with doubts regarding my decision to accept the role. I began to question my ability to perform at the next level of academic rigor and meet the work demands of the counseling position. I would ask myself questions like, "Did I make the right choice?" and "What if I fail?" and "What will my family and friends think about me?" Truthfully, I was scared, but I could not figure out if the root of my fear was the fear of failure or the fear of success.

You know, sometimes you *think* that you are doing the right thing, but you really don't *know* if you are. It's in those situations when you have to be still and let perfect peace begin to speak to your spirit. Don't misunderstand me—it's okay to question yourself. But it's never okay to beat yourself up and torment yourself with negative thoughts. I found out that when faced with difficult times or having to make decisions that can impact your life, we should always wait for peace to show up and then make decisions that align with the peace that we feel. I recommend that you employ the following four steps when making any decision—no matter how big or small it is:

- Quiet yourself.
- Remove yourself from people and their opinions.
- Listen for the voice inside.
- If you don't have peace about it, don't do it.

As I reflected on my decision to accept the assistantship and pursue my master's degree, I felt a great sense of peace about my decision, despite the questions that came to mind. Between going for it and not going for it, peace indicated that moving forward was the right choice, even if it came with challenges. Little did I know that this was one of the best decisions that I would ever make for myself. After completing my master's degree with a near-perfect GPA and experiencing tremendous success as an associate counselor, the university offered me a full-time job as a hall director.

This new position offered me continued professional growth and development, supervisory training, program development, and even opportunities to train other graduate-level counseling students. The role was a perfect opportunity that also set me up to eventually obtain a supervisory position back home in Chicago, working in social services to provide programming and resources for at-risk or underserved youth and families who were dealing with the social ills of poverty, inadequate resources, lack of mental health care, and in need of support and preparation offered by educational and career programs.

The job was a Godsend, preparing me in the present and empowering me later on to be a conduit to provide support and services to families who were dealing with the very same issues and challenges that I had faced as a young boy.

My primary responsibility in the role was to impact the lives of youth through educational and vocational training services. This aspect is so ironic, because I was the kid who grew up without direction, hope, and parental guidance. Now, I am the one providing direction, hope, and, in some cases, parenting skills to youth and families, to help them understand their own purpose and to release their full potential.

A Continual Process

Life is full of twists and turns. The process of going through the passage is ongoing with many pitfalls. We have to learn to trust the process and remain focused, even when we don't fully understand it all. In the end, it brings us to the point that we need to arrive at.

Remember that fear is often based on F.E.A.R. (False Evidence Appearing Real), and it has the capacity to seep into our lives. The presence of fear almost always stifles growth and creates walls of self-containment, with an end result of stagnation, starvation, and death.

Repeat after me, "No fear here!"

Say it again, "No fear here!"

I've shared some of my life experiences, to encourage you and to build confidence in your ability to achieve whatever goals and aspirations that you may have for your own life. Do not be afraid of the process or the unknown. Do not be afraid of change. Do not shy away from the challenges. Do not let the pitfalls intimidate you. Do not be afraid of the journey. Going through the passage is worth it in the end.

Self-Reflection & Life Application

Take a moment and reflect on a personal challenge or struggle that you have faced in your past or may be currently experiencing, then answer the questions below.

1. What made (or makes) this challenge or struggle difficult for you?

   _____
   _____
   _____
   _____
   _____
   _____
   _____
   _____

2. What was (or is) frustrating about this challenge?

   _____
   _____
   _____
   _____
   _____
   _____
   _____
   _____

3. What has been your attitude/approach in dealing with such a challenge? Have you allowed the challenge to become a barrier to your progress?

_____
_____
_____
_____
_____
_____
_____

4. Circle the word that best describes your outlook regarding your struggles the majority of the time.

        PESSIMISTIC   OPTIMISTIC

5. If you circled the word *pessimistic*, what do you think you can do differently to change your perspective or attitude from pessimistic to optimistic?

_____
_____
_____
_____
_____
_____
_____

6. What have you learned about yourself as a result of your personal struggles in life?

_____
_____
_____
_____
_____
_____
_____
_____
_____
_____

7. What mental and emotional growth might have come from your struggles?

_____
_____
_____
_____
_____
_____
_____
_____
_____
_____
_____

8. The chapter talks about the correlation between environmental factors and thinking/behavior, utilizing the illustration of the piranha and the goldfish. Share how environmental factors in your life might be influencing your thinking and behavior.

9. Everyone faces negative factors in their environment, what are some factors that you may be facing at this time?

10. Thinking about these factors, in what ways have they influenced your thinking/behavior? How can someone move forward from those kinds of influences?

11. Think about a personal accomplishment in your life. Do you feel proud of it or have similarly positive feelings about it? If so, share in one to two lines why you feel this way.

12. Before making any decision, no matter how big or small, the chapter recommends that you follow four steps. What are these steps? Why are they important in making decisions in your life?

_____
_____
_____
_____
_____
_____
_____
_____
_____
_____
_____
_____

Reflective Notes

Chapter 2
The Enemy of Excellence Is Average

"Then this Daniel distinguished himself above the governors and satraps, because an excellent spirit was in him; and the king gave thought to setting him over the whole realm."

—Daniel 6:3 (NKJV)

"Don't settle for average. Bring your best to the moment. Then, whether it fails or succeeds, at least you know you gave all you had. We need to live the best that's in us."

—Angela Bassett[11]

Growing up as a kid, average was the norm. As a matter of fact, I don't recall conversations happening around me that were admonishing me to pursue excellence instead of settling for average. The expectations for me that came from the people within my environment was that I was going to be just like everyone around me and experience the same outcomes in life that everyone around me experienced.

Think about the fact that the world population is over 8 billion people and not one person has the same iris or fingerprint or DNA spiral. Just as no two snowflakes are not alike, there is only one you! You are an original! By design, you were set apart, so that your difference or uniqueness would add value to the world.

I find it amazing that the majority of people are either consciously or unconsciously wanting to be a nearly carbon copy of someone else to the world instead of being their original selves. Why would you want to be someone else when you can be you? After all, no other person possesses your exact set of gifts, talents, or abilities, even if they have similar or related ones. This uniqueness that only you possess is what sets you apart from every other person around you and qualifies you as special.

I once heard the late Dr. Myles Munroe say, "When purpose is not known, abuse is evitable."[12]

When we don't understand why we were born or when we don't grasp the concept of a purpose-driven life, we allow our gifts and talents to be misused. Sometimes, if the misuse is bad enough, we're basically (even if it's unknowingly) letting our gifts and talents suffer abuse.

So, to put it simply, we can misuse and even abuse our abilities when we don't understand the purpose according to God's plan for our lives. We can also devalue or diminish our uniqueness by simply being common or refusing to stand out. As a young boy, my insecurities manifested as a result of my childhood trauma. As a result of these insecurities, I felt extremely uncomfortable being different, attempting to stand out, and putting forth my best efforts—so I worked really hard to be status quo or average. But the whole time that I was focused on going down the average road in life, I was unknowingly removing myself from the path of excellence that God called me to operate and display my skills through my uniqueness and individuality during high-stakes situations. Can anyone relate?

The quote by Angela Bassett (at the beginning of this chapter) really resonates with me—because it is challenging you, me, and everyone else to not settle for average. Instead of allowing us to settle, those words encourage us to bring our best to the moment and not shy away from the spotlight that will shine as a result of the best or "excellence" that is on display. In conjunction with her words, I'm a firm believer that the enemy of excellence is average![11]

The enemy of excellence is average, because average thinking forfeits unique abilities to operate in the birthright of excellence—usually out of fear of being rejected, persecuted, or different. It takes courage to be your authentic self and to walk in your individuality. I believe that fear is the number-one reason people settle for what is average instead of showcasing their excellent talent and abilities.

Let's look at an example of courage by a man named Daniel. Daniel was a Jew who had been taken into captivity. Being someone of a younger age at the time, it was decided that he would be given an education by his captors. He excelled in his studies and as a result "made rank" as one of the kingdom's wise men.

In time, the king had an unrestful night, experiencing a dream that troubled and disturbed his ability to sleep. He called for all the magicians, the enchanters, and the Chaldeans to tell him about his dream. The king also issued a firm and unchangeable command that if they did not accurately interpret the dream, then they would be "cut into pieces" and their houses would, essentially, be made a heap of rubbish (see Dan. 2:5 NIV).

According to the dialogue found within the book of Daniel 2:4–11, "The Chaldeans answered the king, and said, 'There is not a man on earth who can tell the king's matter; therefore no king, lord, or ruler has *ever* asked such things of any magician, astrologer, or Chaldean. *It is* a difficult thing that the king requests, and there is no other who can tell it to the king except the gods, whose dwelling is not with flesh'" (Dan. 2:10–11 NKJV).

The king was not satisfied with their response, so a decree went out to kill all the wise men, including Daniel. However, he did not respond out of fear. Instead, Daniel seized the opportunity to trust God with the gifts and talents that had been bestowed upon him. Daniel did not allow fear and the pressure to be average to stop him from displaying excellence through a gift of dream interpretation. The end result was that Daniel accurately interpreted the king's dream and was promoted over the entire province of Babylon as chief governor, to include being over all the wise men of Babylon (see Dan. 2:46–49).

Daniel did not shy away from the moment. Instead, Daniel brought his "best" to the moment. Daniel did not avoid nor shrink back from the opportunity to display excellence, he instead embraced it. The avoidance of excellence is often due to fear. I think that it's important to keep in mind that one way to define fear is by using the acronym F.E.A.R., which stands for "false evidence appearing real." Just for one moment, stop and think about how many of the negative thoughts that we have about ourselves are overall unfounded. There's often no *real* evidence supporting our fears.

Most times, it's only because we "see" images of failure, rejection, hurt, ridicule, or not being good enough that we feel fear. And, because we can easily fall into experiencing such negative imaginations, we often allow the grip of fear (fueled by imagination, not real evidence) to keep us boxed in with an average mindset. I challenge you to resist the fear by refuting the irrational thoughts of failure, rejection, or not being good enough; and then—through positive self-talk—replace these thoughts with images of success.

Say to yourself, "I am different, and my difference makes the difference!"

Say to yourself, "I am fearless! I am powerful! I am a success going somewhere to happen!"

Say to yourself, "I am unique, and my uniqueness is what sets me apart from everyone else in the world!"

I believe that, over time, the negative thoughts can be overcome with the positive thoughts and that you can boldly embrace your gift through self-discovery as well as display your excellence before the world.

Embrace Your Gift through Self-Discovery and Passion

When you are unaware of your purpose, it is extremely difficult to be passionate about anything in life. When you are passionate about something, you have a powerful or compelling emotion or feeling about that specific thing. Passion is the one thing that will fuel the fire within you to push beyond average and enter into a performance level of excellence that will set you apart from others.

If you become passionate about your gifts and talents, you will be compelled to perfect them, and it will take you from good to great, and from great to exceptional. Take sports, for example, you can see a lot of athletes performing the same tasks and having the same shared desires to compete at the highest level in a particular sport.

In every case, there is a small handful of players that will go the extra mile to separate themselves from the rest. This is called passion. This particular athlete is willing to put in extra time, go the extra mile, work harder than everyone else, spend countless hours in the film room, and maintain a life of discipline without supervision. Simply put, this person is in pursuit of excellence and the driver is passion! I recall a time that I was at an event that was held in a public park area, and I couldn't help but notice this young man in the park by himself who was working out. If I had to guess his age, I would say that he was probably somewhere between fourteen and sixteen years old.

I watched this teenager set up his football drill stations, stretch, talk to himself, and then start his workout process. He began to run hills and sprint drills, over and over again, without anyone coaching or motivating him.

This young man was self-motivated about the preparation process to not only get in shape but also to be a great football player. The only time that I observed him resting was to hydrate and stretch. He seemed passionate about separating himself and committed to becoming excellent in his conditioning and route-running skills.

As I thought about what I was witnessing, I believe that this guy was on a mission to separate himself from anybody who was competing against him on the opposite side of the football field. I was so impressed by what I witnessed. I told my wife, "If this kid keeps putting in work like this, when nobody is watching, we will eventually see him one day playing sports in a national league."

> "Be a yardstick of quality. Some people aren't used to an environment where excellence is expected."
>
> —Steve Jobs[13]

My takeaway from the words of Steve Jobs is that you should become the yardstick for yourself and stop looking at others for approval, because they may not come from an environment where excellence is embraced and celebrated. I can personally relate to this quote, because—before my encounter with Mr. Coleman in middle school—nobody within my inner circle had a standard of excellence for themselves, nor did they expect it of me. I had no idea or concept of what excellence was or even looked like.

I also recall a powerful quote that I heard spoken by Dr. Bill Winston as he was preaching a Sunday morning sermon. He was teaching about the story of Daniel and how Daniel embraced his gift and his gift caused elevation and promotion in his life. During the message,

Dr. Winston declared to the audience members, "You are a specialist with no equal."[14] Those seven powerful words take away all excuses for settling for average instead of pursuing excellence in life; they also encourage us to never fear self-discovery while, at the same time, empowering us to embrace our uniqueness and individuality.[14]

When you pursue excellence, you will, by default, begin to set yourself apart from everyone else around you. Your gift (and your way of showcasing your gift) will begin to shine forth, and people will take notice of it. You will go from average to good, from good to great, and from great to excellent!

Your potential is released when you make a decision to press beyond average. Potential is so important because potential is a hidden ability that has a direct link to what you were born or called to do or accomplish.

I want to share a story with you, and it's a true story.

In 1993, Mariah's Storm, a racing filly who was just two years old and had won first place in a recent stakes race, ended up stumbling in her performance at the Alcibiades Stakes, in Lexington, Kentucky, severely breaking the lower portion of one of her front legs. At the time, this kind of break would typically have led to euthanasia—and the filly's racing potential, as well as her life, would have been cut short and left at that. But the owners of Mariah's Storm took a different approach. They decided to go the hard route in hopes of seeing the filly not only recover but also return to racing someday. Not long before her near-fatal fall, she had won the Arlington-Washington Lassie Stakes race.[15]

In 1994, Mariah's Storm placed first in not only the Arlington Oaks Stakes but also the Arlington Matron Stakes. At this point alone, Mariah's Storm had become a record-maker, for having won Arlington Park's three stakes races. As if this incredible feat was not enough, she went on to claim first place in the Turfway Breeders' Cup Stakes the following year. It would not be her last victory.[15]

When she was retired from the track, Mariah's Storm went on to contribute to some of the most well-known names in the horse racing world through being a broodmare; one of her most well-known offspring was Giant's Causeway.[15]

Potential speaks to your destiny!

Average Thinking Is Your Enemy

Average thinking (and behavior) is so dangerous to us because it is inherently limiting. Unfortunately though, average thinking is the average…it takes a conscious effort or a decision on our part to step beyond the limits of average thinking and living.

Most people don't consider what it means to be excellent, much less strive for it. I believe the main reason behind this reality is that excellence requires work. We live in a society where people are seeking success without going through the process that real success requires.

Average-thinking people will put pressure on you to compromise the excellence that is within you. If you continue to remain around average-minded people, the chances are high that you will eventually adopt the same mindset and begin to normalize being common and ordinary in your thoughts and behaviors. Once these patterns are established, they will keep you in a place where you will no longer desire excellence or strive to set a high standard for yourself or others.

When you operate with an average mindset, you could potentially forfeit opportunities to express your unique giftedness. The gift that is on the inside of you has the potential to separate you from others, while commanding the attention of the world! This is why the enemy of excellence is average! If you embrace your talents and cultivate your gift through hard work, you will tap into your potential (hidden ability) and become *unstoppable*!

Nobody can operate in your unique and individual purpose or "assignment." While it is true that different people can perform the same tasks, some individuals are more gifted or talented at performing certain tasks than others. Your specific gifting or ability is uniquely crafted and designed for you and you alone. When you were born, you were made unlike anyone else in the entire universe. When you settle for average instead of striving for excellence, I believe that you deny yourself the opportunity to express your uniqueness.

Potential is on the inside of you, and, as you work out your potential, the world will take notice and begin to celebrate your gift, because your gift makes a difference, and that difference is just what the world is in need of.

Your very existence speaks of your value, worth, and importance, as well as the impact that you were created to make in this world. You could have been born on any date and during any period in the history of this world. However, you were born in this dispensation of time for a specific assignment that has your name on it. You are someone special!

Average thinking can negatively impact a nation academically, socially, politically, spiritually, and economically. Think about the unprecedented crime, failing school systems, and tragic situations that are occurring in our world, even in our great nation. I believe that if a standard of excellence was established in our society, people would have a target to aim for themselves, and it would propel them on a path of personal success.

To Whom Much Is Given, Much Is Required!

If you settle for a life of average, people who look up to you will follow your example of "average" thinking. On the other hand, if you live a life of excellence, people who look up to you will be encouraged to aim for excellence and compromise less with average thinking, because they can watch your life demonstrate that average is the enemy of success. We have a responsibility to pursue excellence, so that we can inspire others to pursue excellence.

I don't believe that anyone was born to be average! Everything and every person is extraordinary in the sense of being unique, different, and exceptional—an "original." Why is every person different? Why did the mold "break" after each and every person was designed? I believe it was to set us all apart, so that each individual person would have equal opportunities to share with the world their unique value and worth, which creates equity for everyone.

Think about the definition of *average* and the definition of *excellent*. *Average* is defined as "not out of the ordinary" or "common,"[16] whereas *excellent* is defined as "very good of its kind," "first-class," or "superior."[17]

Why would you strive to be average? Wouldn't it be so much better to be excellent? Take, for example, the 1990s' championship record of the Chicago Bulls. They were described as "unbeatable," "unstoppable," "unbelievable," and—simply stated—"the best"! The Bulls, in my opinion, set a standard of excellence for all professional sports. They won a total of six World Championship Titles within a single decade (1991 to 1993 and 1996 to 1998). The Chicago Bulls were not an average basketball team; there is no way that you can win three championships back to back twice (for a total of six championships) while playing average basketball!

Their approach to the game was one of dedication, commitment, impeccable work habits, and sacrifice, which translated into excellence! The individual players had to commit to the team goal, which required the mental and physical preparation that was nothing less than excellent. They were not satisfied with just being good or average. The Bulls wanted to be the best team ever, and they proved it during their 1996 season, setting a new NBA single-season record at the time of seventy-two wins, breaking the Los Angeles Lakers' record of sixty-nine, which had been set in the early 1970s.

The Bulls had a hard-work approach to success that can be applied in any aspect of life. The formula that the Bulls used was very simple; go the extra mile, work harder than the other team, remain self-disciplined, give your best effort every time, and never settle for average—strive for excellence!

There is no reward for average, only for excellence. Let's think about the word *excellent* again; remember, it means "very good of its kind," "first-class," and "superior."[17] There's a reason that it gets rewarded.

The contrast between average and excellent reminds me of the story of the prodigal son. When the son came of age, he asked his father for his inheritance, so that he could pursue a lifestyle contrary to his non-average lifestyle. As the story goes on, it tells us that the prodigal son exhausted all of his resources, and, in time, he was no longer the "life of the party."

I can imagine the shame, disgrace, and embarrassment that he must have felt when he was alone and had time to reflect about his decisions and choices. Like so many people, the prodigal son had compromised his value system, self-worth, and potential. Instead of displaying his talents and walking through life in a purpose-driven way, the prodigal son became distracted with fleeting pursuits, such as leaning on popular opinions, gaining acceptance from his peers, and being status-quo. The prodigal son had made a decision to surround himself with "average-thinking" people instead of "exceptional-thinking" people. Exceptional-thinking people are people who dream and think about what's beyond: space travel, entrepreneurship opportunities, writing books, coming up with the cures for life-threatening diseases, and making the world a better place for the next generation of leaders.

After the prodigal son continued down the path of average for so long, he came to his senses and decided to return back to an environment where excellence was the norm. This story reminds me of how, if we are not careful, we can become distracted by a world where average is too often embraced, and we can end up despising the pursuit of excellence.

Sometimes, this "veering off" comes from a place of insecurity: if we think we are not good enough, we may begin a journey of seeking acceptance in all the wrong places.

Average-thinking people can't celebrate exceptional-thinking people. When we embrace our uniqueness, our gifts become like bright lights, shining and bringing separation from "average" accomplishments and results. For better or for worse, an old saying still holds true to this day: *Birds of a feather flock together*. And, most times, they end up in the same place.

Average is not a word that should even be in our vocabulary when it comes to describing our own lives. You've probably heard before that God made your fingerprint completely unique. Did you also know that your voice is unique as well? If you have any doubt that God cares about you and is personally invested in you, let the fact that He gave you such individuality change your perspective.

In fact, when you look at the facts, it begins to feel like everything on the earth is unique, at least where nature is concerned. For example, I heard someone say that there are over 8.7 million different types of living species on the earth and that more are being discovered every day—which is absolutely amazing when you think about it. Every species is different, and this difference is what makes them special. Think about all the sculptures, paintings, songs, books, electronic devices, clothing, cars, houses that we have in society these days. The very thing that makes these different inventions and ideas valuable is the fact that they are all unique in one way or another.

When we attempt to act like someone else, we risk forfeiting the excellence that is displayed through *our* giftedness and individuality. I remember when the "Be like Mike" advertisement by Gatorade came out in 1991.[18] The jingle was fresh and the hook was catchy—you couldn't help but sing along and imagine being like Mike as he dominated the NBA with his high-flying athletic style of play.[18] When you think about what Michael Jordan accomplished both on and off the basketball court, it's no surprise why people would want to be like him. Jordan displayed excellence every time that he stepped onto the basketball court. He outworked his opponents, practiced as if the next game was going to be his last, and left it all out on the floor each time that he played the game. I remember building my schedule around the Chicago Bulls' games, because I wanted to see excellence on display.

When Jordan played basketball in the NBA, the whole world watched with amazement. He played the game with so much trained effort that he made it look easy, and he performed in a spirit of excellence that commanded the attention and respect of the entire world. Jordan became a global icon, and he is the primary reason that the NBA gets the world recognition that it receives to this very day.

Your calling speaks directly to your individuality. For example, identical twins share the same egg in the womb. However, each twin has a specific assignment that speaks directly to their interests, likes, and dislikes. They were conceived from the same egg, yet they are two completely different people, with their own individual dreams, aspirations, and desires. They may have come from the "same place," but they have separate callings, and the individuality bestowed on them enables them to accomplish those callings.

When you look throughout history, you will see how different men and women were called to do different assignments. Some were called to lead, teach, fight wars, or rebuild nations. In all of these situations, the assignments spoke directly to a purpose for being born on the earth, and each and every person that completed their assignment left a mark that will never be erased.

Excellence

You may think that excellence is a very difficult standard to live up to or to achieve. And while it's true that excellence takes effort, the truth is that it also takes effort to operate from a mindset of average thinking.

The story and life of Daniel is a great example of someone who embraced his gifts and talents and did not compromise his assignment. Daniel decided that he was going to be excellent and not average. As a result of his commitment, he was not only promoted but also placed over the entire empire. The Bible says in Daniel 6:3 (NKJV), "Then this Daniel distinguished himself above the governors and satraps, because an excellent spirit *was* in him; and the king gave thought to setting him over the whole realm."

Daniel made a conscious choice to be better than average. He decided that he was going to display a high standard to the world and maintain that standard for himself. Daniel chose to exceed the norm and to be exceptional, even when everyone else around him was just doing the bare minimum. Through diligence and commitment, he positioned himself to be the king's choice!

Like Daniel, we have to make a conscious and deliberate decision to not be "average" with our goals and aspirations, in spite of life challenges. Here are some questions that I've had to work through in my own life, and that I invite you to work through as well:

Will you make excuses and settle for average, or will you do the required work to become excellent?

Do you see yourself as average, and, if so, are you willing to think excellent thoughts about yourself. I challenge you to make daily affirmations about being excellent.

Are you willing to embrace your difference and to allow your difference to make the difference? If so, when?

You must make a decision that mediocrity will only be a past landmark in your journey to a lifestyle of excellence!

Self-Reflection & Life Application

Consider the chapter's discussion on the words *average* and *excellence*, then answer the questions below.

1. In your own words, define *average*.

\
\
\
\
\
\
\
\

2. In your own words, define *excellence*.

3. Why is it important to pursue excellence in life? What are the benefits of allowing excellence to shine forth in your life?

4. Do you consider yourself *average* or *excellent*? Why do you see yourself this way? What examples have you had in your life of average and excellence?

5. If you view yourself as average, what can you do to elevate your thinking so that you can see yourself as living in excellence?

6. List three to five gifts/talents that you believe that you possess that set you apart.

7. Which of these gifts/talents are you currently utilizing and in what capacity?

8. Do you see your gifts or talents elevating you into personal, academic, and/or professional success? If so, how? If not, why?

9. In what ways do you see your abilities being a benefit to others? How can you use your gifts and talents to serve others?

10. It has been said, "Birds of the same feather flock together." What does that mean to you, and how can you apply this principle to your friendships or associations?

11. An accountability partner is a person whom you trust to hold you accountable to achieving specific dreams, goals, or aspirations. Do you have anybody in your circle of friends whom you would consider an accountability partner? If so, name an individual or two and share why you trust them.

12. List three people (current or historical) who inspire you.

13. What character traits do you admire about these individuals?

14. What aspects of their lives would you like to model in your own life?

Reflective Notes

Chapter 3

Personal Image

"We often miss opportunity because it's dressed in overalls and looks like work."

—Thomas A. Edison[19]

When you look in the mirror, what do you see?

Do you see a winner, or do you see a loser?
Do you see confidence, or do you see timidity?
Do you see strength, or do you see weakness?
Do you see growth, or do you see stagnation?
Do you see your past, or do you see your future?

What do you see?

The image that you have of yourself on the inside is what will eventually manifest on the outside. The way that you see yourself directly influences your thoughts, speech, actions, decisions, and, ultimately, your destination.

The image that you have of yourself will become a driving force (or an internal navigation system) that will steer you either onto the path of success or onto the road that leads to failure. Your self-image impacts everything in your life, both good and bad. Another way to say it is that what you imagine for your life will eventually activate to come to pass in your life.

I remember that there was a young man in my old neighborhood who saw himself as a tough guy, and he was more than willing to be a bully while he was at it. Because he saw himself as a troublemaker, everywhere he went, trouble followed (or was already there, waiting on his arrival).

In time, his self-image took him from just being the neighborhood bully to being the neighborhood gang member, then to being the neighborhood criminal. After a while, we didn't see him hanging out on the streets anymore. Later, we found out that he had been arrested and was serving time for armed robbery. After getting out of jail, he went back to the same, criminal lifestyle and was eventually murdered by some people whom he had conflict with.

A tragic end to his life began with an unhealthy view of himself, which included imagining himself as someone he was never made to be. I'm sure that God had better plans for his life, but this guy let his destiny be determined by his self-image. As a result, he became part of a community that paid up in the wages of sin, which God tells us in His Word is death. There is a truth that goes like this, "All those who take the sword will die by the sword" (see Matt. 26:52, WEB). What we want and need to do in life is align ourselves with God's image of us, even when times are difficult, so that we live out the lives that we were created for by Him.

> "You will only go as far as you can see."
>
> —Dr. Bill Winston[14]

When I was going through the different trials and tribulations in my life, I didn't "see" anything beyond them—at least, not initially. You could say that my imagination, at the time, was in "poor performance" mode. In fact, the only thing that I could really imagine about my circumstances was things getting worse and worse.

As time went on, my imaginations (or at least the negative narratives of them) were exactly what manifested in my life. My thoughts were continually in the wrong direction, and they were dragging the story of my life right behind them. What I earned later on in life is that I needed to build boundaries around my thoughtlife, because thoughts paint pictures; and pictures (or images), if unchecked, will dictate your responses; and your responses will become habitual actions.

Once your actions are habitual, they become character traits or a "fixed" mindset that will set the course of your future. I once heard this saying, which is attributed to Lao-Tze:

> Watch your thoughts, they become words.
> Watch your words, they become actions.
> Watch your actions, they become habits.

> Watch your habits, they become character.
> Watch your character, it becomes your destiny.[20]

When you think about this saying, understand that it speaks directly to the power of self-image. What I discovered in life, and something that I hope will benefit you, is that your life outcomes are not dependent on what others see when they look at you as much as they are dependent on what you see when you look at yourself.

So, the million-dollar question is this: What do you see?

You have to be mindful of your thoughts, because your thoughts paint pictures within your heart and these images, whether they are negative or positive, will set the course of your destiny.

Seeing Is Believing

Everything that I acquired in my life came as a result of what I was able to imagine or see in my life. When I had an image of failure and defeat, this is exactly what I experienced in my life. I failed in school, relationships, and daily tasks. The reason why I failed was that I had already seen the end results in my mind, so the outcome was predestined. The images that we have for ourselves is a byproduct of our environments and life experiences.

Environmental factors influence behavior. Remember the story of the piranha and the goldfish? Review chapter one's details about the story, if needed; but the short end of it is that the piranha and goldfish were both placed in a controlled environment to prove a theory that environmental factors influence behavior.

What you see for your life will set the course of actions in your life. Ultimately, your destiny can be changed for the better or worse as a result of the image that you have about yourself. If you see yourself failing, then—the majority of the time—you will fail. If you see yourself as successful, then there's very little that can keep you from experiencing success. This truth is why changing your environment and getting different exposure opportunities is essential for changing the trajectory of your life.

I use the principles of exposure and change of environment to explain the power of imagination to the youth I work with in the S.T.A.R.S. program (a summer program offered by Teen-Train, Inc.). As the interactions occur during S.T.A.R.S., we seek to help the youth remove the walls of containment while expanding their imagination, to help them see themselves as being successful and accomplishing their goals in life.

As established earlier, the way that we view or think about ourselves (inward perception) has a drastic impact on our outlook (outward perception) of the world, opportunities, potential resources, and circle of influence. We have to be careful not to allow our environments (including the people in our environments) to influence or dictate the level of success that we can personally experience or achieve.

What You See Is What You Get

In professional counseling, we use a technique known as cognitive behavioral therapy (CBT), which helps individuals to address negative thought patterns and feelings that influence behavior. Establishing and maintaining a healthy thoughtlife that fosters a strong inward and outward perception of self and the situations that have been faced can be a challenge, but it is worth it.

The images that you see are directly linked to the thoughts in your mind: If you think it, you will see it; and if you see it, you will manifest it. The final outcome can't be separated from the starting point. Whatever thoughts that you have about yourself will play out in your life, because these are the imaginations that ultimately set the course of your actions. The best illustration that I heard that captures this powerful principle and demonstrates the danger of a distorted image is the one of the eagle who saw himself as a chicken.

In the story, an eagle egg rolled down the hill side and ended up in a chicken yard. When the eaglet hatched from the egg, it was surrounded by nothing but chickens. The chickens noticed the immediate difference in this unique and majestic-looking bird. The eaglet, however, didn't see his remarkable difference—he only knew that he was different. As he grew up, he sought acceptance and approval from his chicken environment. The eaglet, basing his worth and abilities on his environment, began to imitate chicken behavior and tried to integrate with the image of being a chicken. The eaglet, like so many people, unknowingly embraced a mindset of limitations because of a distorted image of self that he had internalized. Overtime, the eaglet grew, becoming noticeably different in size, wingspan, and abilities. His differences from the flock generated a lot of negative responses from the chickens, mostly because of their own insecurities, and the eagle began to feel awkward, uncomfortable, and self-conscious. The eagle, like many of us, just wanted to fit in, be accepted, and be approved by his peers. The eagle internalized the rejection and hurt, eventually becoming depressed, withdrawn, ashamed, and confused. The low self-image only compounded his self-esteem issues.

The ongoing emotional threats—whether they stemmed from actual trauma from continued stress and anxiety or simply the perception of the lack of control that he felt, eventually impacted the growing eagle's belief system and sense of self. The end result for the eagle was a state of learned helplessness. The environmental factors facilitated a mindset within him that he couldn't go any further in life than what he could see (or had experienced) right then and there. These factors shaped and framed the eagle's perception of life, self-image, and self-worth until he eventually died in the chicken yard. He never grew into the half of all that he was meant to become. When you compare the differences between an eagle and a chicken, there are obvious and profound differences between the two birds. Check out the following comparison chart.

The Eagle	**The Chicken**
Incredible Vision	Poor Vision
Fearless Nature	Frightened Nature
High-Altitude Flight Ability	Inability to Fly
Vitality (Protected by the Law)	Short Life Span (Popular Menu Item)
Tenacious	Timid
Leader	Follower

When you consider the nature and the God-given characteristics that these two birds possess, the contrast is literally night and day. Chickens are fearful and easily agitated. They run for shelter at the first sight of danger. Eagles, on the other hand, are brave and not easily rattled. For example, when storms come, the eagle will not flee for shelter. Instead, the eagle actually turns his face *into* the storm, to feel the strong wind against his face. Then, at the right time, the eagle will spread his wings, leap off of his perch, and fly directly into the storm. With his wings outstretched, the eagle instinctively catches the violent updrafts caused by the storm, so that he is swept up above the clouds and into the bright sunshine. The eagle will remain above the clouds until the storm blows over and the skies become calm. Now, that's a long way from running around on the ground or being caged up in a barnyard, awaiting the inevitable of being killed, cooked, and served for dinner.

In the story, the eagle's environment framed his self-image, established mental and emotional walls of containment, and ultimately defined his destiny. The tragedy presented within this illustration is that the eagle eventually died in a chicken barnyard without unleashing his God-given potential. The eagle was born to soar freely, to dominate the skies, and to live as the king of the birds. I hope that you keep these key principles in mind as takeaways derived from the story:

- When you can't see yourself as different, you will not do anything differently.
- Your environment sets a mindset that influences the way you see yourself.
- When you don't have a vision, you become stagnant.
- Stagnation stifles creativity and passion.

- Passion will motivate you to work hard.
- Work releases your hidden potential.
- Released potential will take you from good to excellent; and when you operate in excellence, you dominate and set yourself apart from what is average.

To wrap up this section, here are some reminders:

- What you see is what you get!
- You can only go as far as you can see yourself going in life!
- If you can believe it, you will achieve it!
- If you work hard and stay committed to the process, you will obtain your desired goals in life!
- Don't compare yourself to others; be the original whom God created you to be!
- Don't be like the eagle who had the identity crisis and die in a place of self-containment and mental captivity. Instead, be the eagle that you were born to be; soar high and dominate in your sphere of influence.

Identity Crisis

Most people suffer with what I call an identity crisis. Meaning, we don't take time to reflect or think about who we are and what makes us different. As a result, we don't embrace that difference. When you embrace your unique abilities, you begin to tap into your purpose. And when you tap into your purpose, you begin to work out your potential, which catapults you into a class of excellence.

While growing up on the West Side of Chicago in a poverty-stricken community, I could not (initially) see anything more for myself than the negative images around me. As a result of ongoing emotional trauma, continued stress, anxiety, and the lack of control in my life, my cognitive belief system was impacted, sending it down an unhealthy path. My environment did not foster self-efficacy, confidence, and personal success. Consequently, I operated in a state of learned helplessness. I purposely surrounded myself with individuals who shared the same feelings, attitudes, and belief systems. Until we receive "intervention" through someone who cares enough to crack through a shell of wrong beliefs, the fear of failure can be stronger in our life than the desire to succeed.

Think about the above statement for a moment, because it's both true and profound. It wasn't until a man cared enough to encourage changes in my life that I became aware of an opportunity to decide between the fear of failure and the desire for success. I had to settle in my mind and in my heart that if success was my new destination, then I could no longer be fearful of the journey and the work that was required to succeed. There is a movie, "The Last Dragon," by Berry Gordy, that captures the very essence of this concept.[21]

The premise of the movie is that in order to achieve the next level of success, your desire for success has to be greater than your fear of failure. The main character, Leroy Green, was on a personal journey to become a master of kung fu. Leroy completed his final level of training with his grandmaster and was sanctioned to become a master of kung fu. However, Leroy did not feel that he was qualified. He was afraid that he was not good enough, so he continued his quest for more training—out of fear of failure.[21]

Leroy (like myself in real life or the eagle from the story) had a distorted image of himself, and he lacked the necessary confidence to achieve the success that he desired. As Leroy continued along his journey to obtain the "glow" or master's level in kung fu, his desire and will was consistently challenged. Leroy was teased, taunted, and misunderstood, even by his family.[21]

The distorted image that Leroy had of himself drove him to look externally for something that was, all the while, internal (specifically, an image of himself as a master of kung fu). It wasn't until a demand was placed on Leroy's potential through a climactic kung fu battle between him and his archrival, Sho'nuff, that Leroy recognized—and then actualized—the image of a master within himself. Leroy developed confidence in his ability and obtained the "glow" of mastery. Leroy not only won the battle but also gained respect and recognition as a master of kung fu.[21]

Potential Requires Demand

Remember the quote by Lao-Tze (at the beginning of the chapter) and how it expresses that the quality of our thoughts can impact and shape our lives?[20] It reminds us that our ultimate landing point in life all starts with our thoughts, which is why we have to guard our minds and cast down hindering images that we may have of ourselves.

You will follow your most dominant thought!

If you think you can, you will. If you think you can't, you won't. It's that simple! How you think directly impacts the level of success you can obtain in life. The main character in the movie "The Last Dragon" was told by his grandmaster that he was kung fu master material. The very guy who trained him at the highest level of kung fu sanctioned Leroy as a master of kung fu. Yet Leroy didn't think of himself in the same way. My takeaway from this story is that it didn't matter what was said to Leroy, what mattered most was what Leroy was saying to himself—in his thoughtlife.[21]

If you have a distorted image of yourself, this distorted image will shape your words, actions, habits, character, and, finally, your destiny in life. As shared before, I began to realize the power of my thoughts and how my environments influenced my thinking, and I then had a choice: I could keep moving in the wrong direction, or I could shift gears.

I chose the latter, beginning with surrounding myself with positive people and staying away from negative environments. I intentionally surrounded myself with those who wanted to succeed in life and embraced the passage to success.

I challenge you to change your thinking! Get a positive image (picture) for your future in your mind, and then meditate (think about) that image, day and night, until it becomes your reality. Then, your positive thoughts will become your words, actions, and habits. And success will become your final destination in life.

Self-Reflection & Life Application

When you look into the mirror, what do you see?

1. List five adjectives that describe you:

   1. _____

   2. _____

   3. _____

   4. _____

   5. _____

2. If someone were to seek out a character reference about you from your closest friends or family members, what would they say about you?

   _____
   _____
   _____
   _____
   _____
   _____
   _____
   _____
   _____
   _____

3. Name two or three people who are very influential in your life and share why they have such an impact on you.

___

4. In the space below, list the first name of five people from your inner circle. Place a plus sign next to a person's name if you feel that this relationship has a positive influence on your life or a minus sign if you feel that this relationship has a negative influence in your life.

___

5. Reflect on any positive people in your life who are mentioned in the list above, then describe the qualities that they have that you feel makes them a positive influence in your life.

_____
_____
_____
_____
_____
_____
_____
_____
_____

6. If you could take all five of the people listed above and place them into one person, how would you describe that one person? What personal qualities do you share with this "one" person?

_____
_____
_____
_____
_____
_____
_____
_____
_____

7. What impression do you believe that most people have after meeting you?

8. What lasting impression would you want people to have about you?

9. Do you see yourself more like the eagle that was stuck in the chicken yard or more like an eagle that is free to express its full potential?

10. How has your self-image positively or negatively impacted your decision-making and the direction that you have chosen for your life?

11. Identify and list any forms of trauma or stress in your life that may have negatively impacted your self-esteem. Have these situations been resolved or worked through yet? If not, why?

_____
_____
_____
_____
_____
_____
_____
_____

12. If you have negative thoughts about yourself, what are they and what are you doing about them? List the thoughts and your plan of action for addressing them.

_____
_____
_____
_____
_____
_____
_____
_____

13. List two or three people whom you can talk openly and honestly with about your thoughts and feelings without feeling judged.

Reflective Notes

Chapter 4

Attitude, the Key to Success

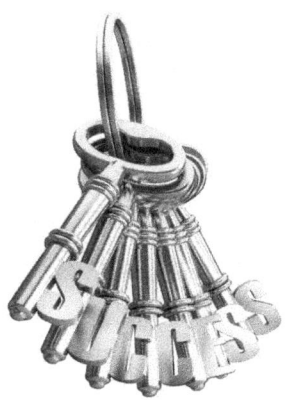

"A positive attitude causes a chain reaction of positive thoughts, events, and outcomes. It is a catalyst, and it sparks extraordinary results."

—Wade Boggs, retired professional baseball player[22]

"Choosing to be positive and having a grateful attitude is going to determine how you're going to live your life."

—Joel Osteen, pastor[23]

"Ability is what you are capable of doing. Motivation determines what you do. Attitude determines how well you do it."

—Raymond Chandler, novelist[24]

"Develop an attitude of gratitude, and give thanks for everything that happens to you, knowing that every step forward is a step toward achieving something bigger and better than your current situation."

—Brian Tracy, motivational speaker[25]

"Your attitude, not your aptitude, will determine your altitude."

—Zig Ziglar, motivational speaker[26]

I shared a list of quotes that communicate the significance and importance of having the right attitude. The one quote that resonates with me the most is the one by Wade Boggs. Let's look at that one again: "A positive attitude causes a chain reaction of positive thoughts, events, and outcomes. It is a catalyst, and it sparks extraordinary results."[22]

The reason that this quote resonates so much with me is because I experienced firsthand the impact of having a bad attitude and how it created a vacuum-like effect in my life—an effect that spiraled into "a chain reaction of thoughts, events, and outcomes"[22] that I regretted later on in life. What I learned, in essence, is that attitude is a little thing that makes a big difference in every area of your life. I've already shared a lot about how the wrong attitude can lead to negative impact. What about the right attitude though? When you have the right attitude, you position yourself for these three things to happen:

- Recognition
- Promotion
- Influence

Do you remember the story of Joseph? It's probably the best example of someone who was granted recognition, promotion, and influence as a result of maintaining the right attitude while facing trials and tribulations. To recap, God gave Joseph a vision (or a dream) as a youth that he would be sought out by others and that he would be in a position of great power and influence. As the youngest of his many brothers, "group leader" wasn't exactly a title that Joseph was lined up for, especially from a cultural perspective. In fact, when Joseph shared his dream with his family (out of his apparent immaturity at the time), his brothers despised him and his father rebuked him. Following these incidents would be major changes in Joseph's life (partly thanks to the animosity from his brothers) that would grow him up. Although the events and circumstances that he faced, which included being sold into slavery, were very difficult, the account that we read in the book of Genesis suggests that, somewhere along the way, Joseph chose the right attitude. As unlikely as his "lot in life" suggested that the sun would ever shine upon his personal circumstances, Joseph's decision to live in excellence eventually led him from a position of slavery to oversight. In the end, his dream came to pass.

It's likely that the rejection and ridicule Joseph faced was devastating and had some kind of negative impact on his attitude and confidence that the dream would come to pass in his life, at least initially. But even if they did, Joseph didn't stay in the negative. He shifted to the positive, to the excellent. The right attitude has the power to change the trajectory of your life forever.

Attitude is a belief system that will govern your actions. I believe that the more that Joseph talked (or thought) about his dream, the stronger his belief became that he could one day rule and govern and that he could see himself as a person of great influence. Perhaps the greatest tip off in the story that Joseph was holding onto hope of seeing the vision manifest was that, while still in prison (for a crime that he did not commit), Joseph asked an acquaintance to tell the leader of the land about him. Think about the boldness of that request! I don't believe that such boldness was developed overnight. Despite years of rejection and mistreatment, Joseph demonstrated boldness as a result of who he chose to become. During challenging moments, Joseph's mind was probably flooded with invitations to reset his belief system to adopt and conform to an attitude of failure, defeat, and despair.

As the story progresses and Joseph keeps taking the higher road, we see that God continually provided protection, gave favor, and blessed the works of Joseph's hands. If we fast-forward the story, you can see by the end of Genesis chapter forty-one that Joseph has been totally exonerated and placed into the second-highest seat of recognition, power, and influence over all of Egypt and was known throughout the world. To put it simply, he went through the passage.

When I think about the story of Joseph and all the people (past and present) who did not allow personal hardships to change how they personally saw themselves as leaders, change agents, and those making a positive contribution to the world, it encourages me to have the right attitude.

The greatest individuals share these things in common:

- Each has experienced tremendous adversity in their efforts to manifest their vision and operate in their areas of giftedness.

- Not one of them folded under pressure. Instead, they met the pressure head on and maintained a victorious attitude (as a result, they were promoted in their respective areas and received recognition, power, and influence).
- As a result of what they believed about themselves, we read about them today in our history books.

Speaking of great individuals, perhaps Winston Churchill said it best, "Attitude is a little thing that makes a big difference."[27] Your attitude is a part of your belief system, and your belief system will dictate what you believe about yourself!

What is your attitude or belief system, and how does it impact how you think about yourself? Take a moment and reflect about what you believe about yourself, then ask yourself if you might need an attitude adjustment.

Do You Have the Right Attitude?

Everyone has been told at one time or another that they needed an attitude adjustment. Honestly speaking, we all can benefit from a little attitude adjustment every now and then. But how often are we really paying attention or following through on this reality?

Think about the fact that we get our cars checked out every 3,000 or 10,000 miles for oil changes. Or that we have routine service work done in our homes when recommended by service technicians or similarly trusted resources. Or that, if our bodies are feeling challenged, we schedule a doctor's appointment to receive a checkup.

However, when we need an attitude adjustment, even when it's pointed out by others, the tendency for many is to respond in one of three ways, if not all three:

We don't feel like there is anything wrong with our attitude, and we stop there. As a result, we feel no need for an attitude adjustment.

We perceive criticism. As a result of something being made known as needing to change, we can take offense.

We become defensive. As a result, we can become combative (and might even refuse to change *even when we see the need to change*).

When we refuse to adjust our attitude, we become unteachable and the end result is often missed opportunities for personal growth and development.

> "The greatest day in your life and mine is when we take total responsibility for our attitudes. That's the day we truly grow up."
>
> —John C. Maxwell[28]

I appreciate the connection that John Maxwell made in regards to us taking personal responsibility for our attitudes and maturity.[28] If you have been told that you need an attitude adjustment in order to grow to the next level in life yet refuse to take heed, then you lack maturity and are refusing to grow up. This type of mindset or attitude is counterproductive to forward progress and success.

When you deny yourself the opportunity for growth and maturity, you create obstacles and hindrances that can potentially delay your success or cause you to forfeit it altogether. On the other hand, if you open your heart and mind to receive constructive criticism and then make a conscious effort to change, it is a sign of maturity that will ultimately lead to promotion, recognition, and power.

Attitude is heard in your speech, seen in your appearance, and observed in your actions. People who refuse to take responsibility for their attitudes are perceived as immature individuals. An immature attitude feeds into a self-defeated mindset that is controlled and manipulated by external factors.

When a leader has the right attitude, everyone benefits. Consider what Proverbs 29:2 (WEB) says, "When the righteous thrive, the people rejoice; but when the wicked rule, the people groan." This verse is conveying that when good people run things—people with the right attitude—everyone is glad (or can benefit from this type of leadership because, in a way, everyone wins, including the leader). In contrast, when a ruler or leader is bad (whether *bad* gets defined as controlling, insecure, fearful, oppressive, insensitive, or prejudiced), everyone groans or is sad. Probably all of us have—at some point—heard it said that "with great power comes great responsibility." But these words are not just a saying, they are a reality! It is essential for anyone in a position of influence, power, and leadership to have the right attitude. One of the primary character traits of an effective leadership is having an attitude that says, "I never lose, I only learn."

Attitude Alignment

Properly aligned steering is important to the safety and proper functioning of your vehicle. If you've ever driven a vehicle with a misalignment, then you know exactly what I mean! Beyond offering frustration and requiring extra effort to drive until it is fixed, a car that has severe misalignment is potentially dangerous and can suffer excessive wear and tear to tires, brakes, bearings, etc.

Just like you can instantly tell when a car really needs a wheel alignment, people can usually tell when you need an attitude alignment. Long after your presence is gone, your attitude is still felt, whether good or bad. It is important to understand that your attitude can show up before you and usually remains after your departure.

You can ask any random person, "Do you need an attitude adjustment?" and, nine out of ten times, the answer would be, "I don't have an attitude problem. I'm good!" Is that what your response would be as well?

Once the pressures of life come (be it academics, work-related scenarios, financial situations, or relational challenges), a person's posture, outlook, speech, mindset, and sometimes moral stance may change…and not for the better. When a negative change happens, the reason why is that the individual really did not have the right attitude (outlook about their situation) to begin with, and the pressure of a situation or circumstance is exposing someone's otherwise hidden attitudes. Your attitude can place you on a trajectory of forward progress or bring you to a complete halt. Thomas Jefferson said it this way: "Nothing can stop the man with the right mental attitude from achieving his goal; nothing on earth can help the man with the wrong mental attitude."[29]

Your attitude affects every area of your life, including how you deal with people, situations, and circumstances. Let's look at the legendary Michael Jordan for the sake of this point. Jordan arguably is the greatest basketball player to ever wear gym shoes. In my field of profession, I work with all generations and I find it interesting that even those of Gen Z, who were not even *born* during the Michael Jordan championship years, mostly agree that Michael Jordan is the best to have ever played basketball (although, understandably, they seem to be more familiar with LeBron James and other athletes closer in age to their own generation). But for all the fame and success that he has known across decades, did you know that Michael "Air" Jordan, in 1978, tried out for the varsity basketball team at Laney High School in Wilmington, North Carolina, *and did not make the roster*?[30]

What if Jordan had allowed that one experience to negatively impact his attitude about the game of basketball and just said to himself, "Maybe I'm not as good as I thought"…or, "I can't compete in this game at the next level"…or, "Maybe basketball is not the sport for me"…? It would have changed history.

Jordan did not adopt a defeated attitude. Instead, he worked harder and remained committed to the process of hard work until his game improved, both offensively and defensively. He also grew a few more inches during the off season and returned the next season to claim a starting position on the basketball team. And the rest is history!

Everything Starts and Ends with Your Attitude

As a youngster, I did not realize at first how important my attitude was to myself and others. I did not realize that people could sense my attitude, whether good or bad. People responded to me based on the attitude I displayed. My siblings and I endured a lot of emotional hardships growing up. We had to face a lot of challenges at an early age, especially after the death of our parents. However, we all had to learn for ourselves the reality of how "attitude…will determine your altitude."[26] (As mentioned previously, Mr. Coleman was hugely instrumental in helping me step toward the right attitude!)

Once I embraced the idea of excellence and seeing myself as successful in life, I began to shape my future with my thoughts, words, actions, and habits, all of which testified to my attitude. At the time, I didn't know about the power of positive self-talk, but I did it. As a therapist today, I understand the importance and impact of the words that I released over myself. I would make the following declarations over myself daily:

- "I can do anything that I set my mind to do!"
- "I can be anything that I set my mind to become!"
- "I am not defined by my situations and circumstances!"
- "Nobody can hold me down!"
- "Failure is not an option for me!"
- "I will accomplish my goals!"
- "I will not allow fear to contain me!"
- "Nothing can stop me!"

- "I will be successful!"
- "I am unstoppable!"

I learned at an early age that my attitude was a key factor to my success and reaching my destiny. Having an "always-learn, never-lose" attitude began to open doors and attract the right people in my life. A good attitude will not only open doors, it will get you a seat at the table. Likewise, having a bad or losing attitude will keep doors closed and prohibit new opportunities from manifesting in your life.

When there were times that I didn't have all the credentials or the maximum work experience but still advanced forward as opportunities arose, I would often ask what the determining factor of choosing me was. The response that I most often received was that I presented myself as teachable and that my outlook about any challenges that the job or task may have presented was always optimistic.

I was not always the smartest or most qualified person; however, I always had an attitude of "I can do anything if given the opportunity, understanding, and support." I am thoroughly convinced that 75 percent of my success has been a direct result of my win-win, "never-lose, only-learn" attitude in life.

> "People may hear your words, but they feel your attitude."
> —John C. Maxwell[31]

Looking back at my life, I see how attitude, when combined with effort, opened many doors for me.

When I obtained my first job in high school, a comment that I often heard was that my attitude was right for the job. I did not have any work experience, I just had the right attitude.

When I was in college, I joined a fraternity, and the brothers told me on a regular basis that, having the right attitude to be a leader, I should pursue leadership within it. Following their advice, I became the chapter president and, later on, the graduate advisor for the chapter.

When I decided to attend graduate school at Eastern Illinois University, I applied for a graduate assistantship position in the housing department. While I was excited about the possibility, I was also somewhat nervous because I lacked experience! During the interview, though, I remained positive, focused, optimistic, and ready to take advantage of a great opportunity. Although I overall felt comfortable and confident, I didn't know what the final outcome would be. Throughout the interview, I kept hearing questions that referenced my transferable skills and work-related experience for the position. The selection process was very competitive, and there was a big pool of candidates for only five available graduate assistantship positions.

At the conclusion of my interview, I thanked everyone for their time, and I expressed a sincere gratitude for the opportunity of a lifetime. I also shared why I was the best candidate for the position. My attitude remained positive before, during, and after the interview process. After a much-anticipated wait, I was notified that I had gotten the job!

After starting my new position, my supervisor informed me that my interview was "awesome." He also pointed out the fact that my lack of experience showed during my interview. However, the determining factor for the search committee's decision to hire me was an outstanding attitude. Other candidates had more relevant work experience, but I had what was described as a "teachable attitude," which was the quintessential ingredient for the job.

As you go through life, remember:

- The right attitude will open doors for you that experience alone cannot and will not open.
- The right attitude can separate you from the pack and elevate you to the top.
- The right attitude has the potential to cause rules and regulations to change on your behalf.
- The right attitude is the key to your success!

The graduate assistantship gave me an income, a path to a debt-free master's degree, and supervisory experience. It also honed my administrative abilities and professional counseling skills—ones that I use to this very day when serving students, families, and clients. But the assistantship didn't (and wouldn't have) come to me as a result of me having a bad attitude. It came my way because I let a right attitude position me to receive it. The right attitude creates the right opportunities that then set the trajectory of our lives.

Attitude Affects Vision

I once heard a story about a man who was intrigued as he walked past a construction site. So, he stopped and inquired about the site. He wanted to know what the end product would be. The first construction worker nonchalantly replied, "I'm just laying bricks for a building." The gentleman saw another guy working at the same construction site, one who was singing and smiling. So, the gentleman inquired again about the project. Surprisingly, the response was different. This construction worker shared that he is laying bricks for a state-of-the-art, multi-purpose facility that will house orphans, homeless people, and victims of domestic violence. He shared that this facility will provide educational and vocational training programs, computer classes, and Sunday church services. The second construction worker was so excited to talk about the opportunity he had to be a part of the building blocks of an amazing vision to help change the lives of people for the better.

After walking away from the site, the gentleman reflected on the distinctly different accounts of the same project: two people at the same site held two totally different perspectives about the end product. The difference between the perspectives was the attitude toward the role being played in the overall project. One construction worker only saw the project as a typical day on the job while earning a living. Meanwhile, the other worker viewed this opportunity as a chance to be a part of a great vision to impact a community.

The construction worker who had the attitude of excitement could clearly see the vision and how his skills were contributing to the lives of others while the other construction worker, hindered by his attitude, could not see beyond the job. You must be cognizant of the fact that your attitude affects your ability to see (vision) and that without vision you will unconsciously minimize your role and fail to see your significance in the big picture.

As Zig Ziglar put it so well, someone's attitude will also determine that person's altitude![26] So, remember that if you want to fly high in life, it's imperative to have the right attitude. You will only go as high in life as your attitude allows you to go. Don't let a little thing (attitude) stop you from experiencing a big future (success, joy, prosperity, and satisfaction).

Self-Reflection & Life Application

Review the quotes at the beginning of chapter four, then answer the questions below.

1. Which of the quotes resonates with you the most? Write it down and share why its impact is the greatest to you.

   _____
   _____
   _____
   _____
   _____
   _____
   _____
   _____

2. Now, write your own positive quote or personal affirmation that will help you shift mentally when needed and maintain a positive attitude and perspective about your life.

   _____
   _____
   _____
   _____
   _____
   _____
   _____
   _____

3. When you have the right attitude, you position yourself for three things to happen in your life. What are these three things?

   1.

   2.

   3.

4. How do you think these three things can make your life more fulfilling?

5. Who is one of your role models? What type of attitude does this individual have about life?

6. What is one adversity that he or she had to overcome to achieve success? Please explain in detail.

7. Has anyone ever told you that you should improve your attitude? Please explain why you think this is said to you.

8. How do you feel about your own attitude? Please explain in detail.

_____
_____
_____
_____
_____
_____
_____
_____

9. Do you have a mindset that is open toward correction and constructive feedback?

               YES   NO

10. Do you agree with this statement, "People who refuse to take responsibility for their attitudes lack maturity"? Why or why not?

_____
_____
_____
_____
_____
_____
_____
_____

11. Have you ever had a teammate, classmate, or coworker with a really bad attitude? How did the attitude of this individual impact your attitude?

12. How would you support or encourage a friend or family member who had a really bad attitude? What advice would you offer this person to help improve his or her attitude?

Tips for Overcoming a Negative Attitude

When you start to feel pressure and stress, do you notice that your attitude changes? Do you become more irritable? If so, please see the tips below on how to overcome a negative attitude:

- Think positive and stay positive.
- Find something inspirational, such as a quote, poem, or song, that helps to change your attitude (then say, recite, or sing it to yourself).
- Think about something that makes you happy.
- Surround yourself with positive people and hang out with them.
- Focus on the message and not the tune.
- See yourself as victorious!
- Look for an opportunity to serve others.
- Remind yourself that you are a work in progress.
- Find humor in every situation.
- Laugh at yourself.
- Be thankful.
- Stay away from "chicken" talk!
- And always remember the three *R*s:
    1. Relax
    2. Reflect
    3. Release
- Use first-person statements to help yourself stay encouraged while developing a positive attitude, such as:

"I can do anything!"

"I can be anything!"

"I am not defined by situations, circumstances, or people!"

"I cannot fail!"

"I will have a good attitude!"

"I will be successful!"

"I will not allow fear to contain me!"

"I am unstoppable!"

"I will not allow a negative experience to shape or influence me from thinking positively about myself and my future."

Positive Attitude Principle (PAP)

In order to maintain a positive attitude, you have to establish boundaries and rules of engagement for yourself when dealing with life challenges and conflict. I recommend using my Positive Attitude Principle (PAP) to help you navigate these spaces, while maintaining a positive attitude:

- Think about what you could have done differently that could have impacted the outcome of the situation in a positive way so that your character is not compromised.
- Step away from the situation momentarily to regroup emotionally before engaging the situation. This will allow cooler heads to prevail and opportunity for introspection and reflection.
- Listen for understanding and don't make assumptions.
- Think the best, not the worst.
- Own your impact.

Apply the PAP while reading the scenarios below and respond to the questions.

Individual Scenario

Patricia was new in town and was invited to a social event by her close and dear friend Maria, whom she had known before moving to the area. When Maria and Patricia arrived at the event, Maria wandered off to talk and socialize with other friends and never returned to check on Patricia. After a couple of hours of being alone and becoming overwhelmed with frustration and disappointment, Patricia decided to leave the event and go home.

If you were Patricia, how would you express your feelings about this situation to Maria in a way that would set the tone for positive growth?

Group Scenario

Terrell is the assigned leader of a study group in his class. The group agreed to meet weekly in preparation for their paper and presentation for class. After the first meeting, the group decided to divide up and share responsibilities among all the team members.

Terrell began to notice that nobody in the group was fulfilling their responsibilities, with the exception of himself and one other teammate. The group has less than two weeks to complete the project before the mandatory deadline. Fifty percent of the grade is to be based on synergy (teamwork) and the remaining 50 percent is to be based on the research paper.

What attitude should Terrell have? How would you advise Terrell to successfully motivate his group to complete the project and meet their deadline as a team?

Reflective Notes

Chapter 5

Putting the Picture Together
(The Power of Finished Work)

"When we make progress quickly, it feeds our emotions. Then, when there's a period of waiting or we hit a plateau, we find out how committed we really are and whether we're going to see things through to the finish or quit."

—Joyce Meyer[32]

What Joyce Meyer is basically asking you and me in the above quote is, "Can you stand the rain?"[32] The rain that I'm referring to is the less-than-ideal conditions that we face—can you hold on long enough to withstand the twists and turns, ups and downs, and highs and lows of life without giving up on your dreams? Before you answer that question, realize that there are three questions "within" that one, and those are:

- Will you remain committed?
- Will you stay the course?
- Will you finish what you started?

Starting something is the first step in the direction of finishing. The principle of finishing what you start is embraced by successful people who are in all walks of life: business, sports, media, technology, politics, ministry, and entertainment.

Commitment is the quintessential ingredient that is required to finish anything that you start. Take, for example, the writing of a book, the starting of a business, the beginning of a lifestyle of fitness, or the building of a successful marriage. In each one of these cases, you have to take action in order to start in the direction of your end goal.

Desiring something is one thing, but taking action to obtain that which you desire requires courage, will, and the risk of failure. Starting something can be a challenge, but like Zig Ziglar said, "You don't have to be great to start, but you have to start to be great."[33] The real question is: Are you willing to be great? If so, you will have to "start" in order to pursue greatness.

Are You Willing to Be Great?

The journey or road to greatness can sometimes be a scary and lonely journey. Along the way, you will have to fight through doubt and negative self-talk, such as questions like, "What if I fail?" or "What will people say about me?" These sorts of thoughts, which are laced with fear, can cause you to shrink away and forfeit the journey before you even take your first step.

Fear can make you question yourself and, as a result, stop your forward progress. I count fear as one of the greatest enemies to your progress and to the belief that you can finish what you started.

Belief is a powerful force, and if fear can convince you to believe that you *can't* accomplish something, then you will, most of the time (if not always), fail in your efforts. On the other hand, fear knows that if you ever develop the belief that you can achieve your goals in life, then very little (if anything) on earth can stop you from finishing what you started.

Once you believe that you can accomplish something, you will develop *confidence*, *grit*, and *perseverance* that will build the capacity for you to finish what you set out to accomplish. As you make up your mind to finish what you start, you then become a finisher in life. Being a finisher is an attitude and a mindset that says that you are willing to go through the struggle in order to make the necessary progress in life.

> "If there is no struggle, there is no progress."
> —Frederick Douglass[34]

Do you remember the commercial mentioned at the beginning of this book? It was the Nike commercial starring Michael Jordan that was entitled "Failure" and aired during Jordan's playing years with the Chicago Bulls. I bring it back up because it's such a great example of confidence, grit, and perseverance. The commercial doesn't show Michael talking to the press or playing basketball; it shows Michael

Jordan pulling into the United Center before a game and getting out of his vehicle. While walking through the hallways, Jordan began to reflect on his past failures. As mentioned previously, the commercial concludes with Jordan making this very powerful statement, "I've failed over, and over, and over again in my life, and that is why I succeed." He was summing up his passage to success—by saying that his success came through his trials and struggles of having to overcome failure. The words that Jordan spoke also reveal that his greatness didn't come overnight. His greatness was the byproduct of him starting and then never giving up on himself as a basketball player.[2]

Jordan did not allow his failures to stop his drive to succeed. Instead, he used that disappointment to fuel his desire to never give up. Jordan, like anyone else who has achieved anything great in life, understood the value and importance of not allowing a setback to stop him from finishing the work that was started.

He did not allow defeat to stop him in his quest for greatness. Jordan, in the journey to all his success, had to outlast failure long enough to succeed. He, like so many others, had to endure the season of failure and potential ridicule in order to develop the skills and confidence necessary to live at the winning level. On the other side of failure is success!

Former President Nixon said, "A man is not finished when he's defeated. He's finished when he quits."[35] My takeaway from these words is that failure or defeat is not the final say so when it comes to progress. Your decision to quit or give up is what stops your forward progress and, ultimately, denies you the joy of finishing what you started.

After you start your passage in life, chances are, you will hit a plateau (sometimes sooner than later). During this plateau or moment, you will find out how committed you really are and whether you are going to stay the course and FINISH what you started.

In order to finish anything that you start, you will have to commit to the journey that comes with the passage. The journey usually offers at least a few uncomfortable times along the way, because it requires patience, mental toughness, and the willingness to risk failure. The passage is a time when there is no fanfare, lights, or cameras—only action! These are moments when it's only you and your dreams.

Navigating the passage brings with it moments of silence, time for personal reflection, introspection, and life adjustments when needed. Such moments are really private (yet "in your face"), self-check seasons, where development of character, image, integrity, attitude, will, desire, and commitment is available. In my opinion, the passage is necessary and extremely important, because it is a transformational time that will determine your level of success or depth of failure.

The Wilderness

The passage is much like a modern-day wilderness experience. It is designed to expose what's in our hearts and thought life while preparing us for the next level of success. We all need a wilderness experience so that we can know what's in our hearts.

When we understand what's in our hearts, we can address otherwise-hidden issues and grow individually, professionally, relationally, and spiritually. This process helps to fortify and qualify us for promotion in life. Think about the life of Joseph. He had to endure hardship while simultaneously embracing personal-growth situations, so that he would ultimately be in position to finish or fulfill the dream that God had given him.

The wilderness is an undesirable place, according to the average-thinking mindset. After all, it can be a very uncomfortable and sometimes shameful experience. However, it is necessary for a purging process, which yields growth, grit, endurance, commitment, and perseverance. The wildernesses of the passage empower you with the mettle and mindset to finish the work—if you let them!

A wilderness experience also allows you to come face-to-face with your hidden heart issues, and it provides an opportunity to deal with your issues without shame. A wilderness experience is a personal, self-check season in your life. By the way, I'm pretty sure that Michael Jordan—as well as others who have experienced any level of success over time—encountered personal-wilderness experiences. Everyone has plenty of opportunities to give up, to embrace unforgiveness or to quit on life, especially when things are not going as planned. While on your passage, you will make the decision to either quit or finish what you started.

Finished Work or Unfinished Work… What Will Be Your Legacy?

I believe that every person has a desire to fulfill their dreams, because you were born to finish! You were born to win in life! The blueprint for success is within you, and work and commitment to the process provides the opportunity to manifest your potential from the inside out. You have dreams that you want to fulfill and, more importantly, a work that is required to bring that dream to fruition! You have purpose and potential on the inside of you.

It's your responsibility to start and finish your race, so that you can leave a legacy of success, fulfillment, endurance, courage, faith, integrity, and commitment; a legacy of finishing what you start.

Will your legacy be one of finished work or unfinished work? When people talk about you, will they say that you are the type of person who starts things and never finishes? Or will they say that you are the type of person who locks in, stays focused, and doesn't quit until you have completed what you started? My motto is this: If I can start it, then I am equipped to finish it!

Become a Graveyard Digger

When I was in my senior year of high school, I remember having one of those father-son type of conversations with my Uncle Frank regarding my future plans. He asked me what I wanted to be and what my purpose was for wanting to attend college. My response was that I wanted to become a lawyer or businessman or something of that sort in life. I wasn't 100 percent sure of my career pathway after high school, I just knew that I wanted to attend college away from home.

To my surprise, my uncle's response was, "Why…Why would you want to go to college to become a lawyer or business person? That's a lot of trouble!" The message from his end included a perspective that those types of jobs are too stressful as well as questioning why anyone would want that for a life. He continued by saying, "Lawyers get caught in too much mess! They are corrupt, and they don't make enough money to have to deal with other people and their problems! Why don't you just skip college and get a job like me? Earn some good, honest money working at the graveyard! Dwayne, what you are talking about is not realistic for black people. Become a graveyard digger!"

My uncle didn't mean any harm when he tried to convince me to forfeit an opportunity to attend college and instead pursue a full-time job working at the cemetery with him. He was just speaking out of his own personal "barnyard" experience. The irony of the situation is that I wanted to get out into the world and be around people who were pursuing hopes and living out their dreams, yet my uncle was trying to convince me to remain in a place of starvation, stagnation, and death—the graveyard!

I once heard Dr. Myles Munroe talk about how the graveyard was the richest place on earth because of the wasted gifts, talents, and dreams that were never actualized; to summarize his words, the graveyard is a place filled with unwritten books, unfulfilled visions, forgotten aspirations, and ignored potential.[36] I did not want to be a contributor to this already-rich place that was filled with untapped possibilities; therefore, I decided against my uncle's advice, choosing instead to pursue college after graduating from high school and finish my quest to be a first-generation college graduate.

The conversation with my uncle taught me a great lesson. It helped me to understand that you must be careful, mindful, and observant of whom you share your dreams with. A person can be a loved one, coworker, or close friend who genuinely has your best interest at heart, however, you should never underestimate the power of unfinished work. People who made the decision to quit while going through the wilderness experience have a tendency to speak from that place of reference. Don't get angry with them; just understand their mindset, so that you don't allow their perspective to stop your forward progress.

My parents had died when I was a kid, and—as a result of that void in my life—I never had the opportunity to witness them fulfilling their dreams and finishing up tasks that they set out to accomplish. Unfinished work often leads to more unfinished work. Whenever I felt depressed, devalued, worthless, or insignificant, it was a direct result of not understanding my purpose and how important and impactful diligence, commitment, focus, and finished work are to my self-image. To every parent who reads this book, please model for your children what you want them to experience in their lives. If you display a lifestyle of diligence, integrity, and finishing what you start, your children will adopt this very mindset and workstyle for themselves. They will follow your example of "finished work."

Finish the Work

Unfinished work looks just like an image of a puzzle with pieces missing. There is no real appreciation for the picture, because the image is distorted due to the fact that there are missing pieces. If a puzzle is not finished, the picture is incomplete; if the picture is incomplete, it has lessened value or worth. Just like the puzzle that holds lessened value because of the missing pieces, our personal lives can appear to be without lasting impact when we do not finish our work. The best thing that you can do for yourself (and others) is finish what you started. You've got what it takes to finish it, so go to it.

Playing to Win

When I was a youngster, winning meant everything to me. When I began to play organized sports, though, I learned that it wasn't about winning or losing; it was about learning sportsmanship, discipline, and teamwork. This realization translated into winning in life instead of just winning a game. As you prepare yourself mentally, put in the work, be disciplined and committed with the right attitude, you will win in life, because winning starts with finishing what you start.

When I decided to run the Chicago Rock-n-Roll half-marathon (13.1 miles), I was not competing to come in first place or to break records. I didn't even match my personal training course time. However, I still felt extremely proud and accomplished—because I finished the race. (And now I can tell other people that I'm a marathon-finisher!)

> "Perseverance is not a long race; it's many short races one after the other."
>
> —Walter Elliot[37]

Because small victories eventually lead to big victories, I preserved through the rigorous training schedule and dietary restrictions in preparation for the marathon. I encourage you to utilize positive self-talk while going from victory to victory in your life. Stay the course, and continue to speak the following positive declarations over yourself:

- I am victorious!
- I am a winner!
- I am a finisher!
- I will complete what I started!

Keep in mind that when I speak about winning, I am talking about you finishing any work or tasks that you have started. The work can be graduating from high school, completing a certificate program, graduating from college (or graduate school), pursuing the career of your dreams, starting a business, being a better parent, being a better spouse, starting a church, or writing a book. Whatever fulfills you and adds quality of life to those around you links you directly to your purpose, your calling, your assignment, and your work.

Discovery of Self Leads to Discovery for Others

I remember looking into the eyes of my GED students from my educational and vocational programs and seeing confidence, pride, joy, fulfillment, growth, and accomplishment—finished work! These students were elated and excited about their futures. Why? Because another piece of the puzzle was now in place, and they were actualizing their dreams. They began to share with me how they planned to attend college or trade school in order to better prepare themselves for the next level of work in their lives.

> "The difference between a successful person and others is not lack of strength, not lack of knowledge, but rather a lack in will."
>
> —Vince Lombardi[38]

Never forget, it's not the lack of strength, nor the lack of knowledge, but the lack of will that can delay or deny you along your passage to personal success and fulfillment in life. I challenge you to set your mind to finish what you start, and like Nike said, "Just do it!"[39]

Self-Reflection & Life Application

Frederick Douglass said that "If there is no struggle, there is no progress."[34]

Consider that quote for a moment. Also consider where there have been struggles in your own life, then answer the questions below.

1. The chapter says that "failure is the other side of success." What does this mean to you?

   _____
   _____
   _____
   _____
   _____
   _____
   _____

2. Is it challenging for you to make and keep personal/professional commitments, such as meeting deadlines and completing projects? Why or why not?

   _____
   _____
   _____
   _____
   _____
   _____
   _____

3. Michael Jordan said, "I've failed over, and over, and over again in my life, and that is why I succeed."[2] Why is this message significant, and how can you apply this principle to your life?

4. List three tasks/challenges that you believed that you failed at in your life.

5. Reflecting on your failures, what have you learned about yourself and how can you turn these experiences with failure into experiences of success?

_____
_____
_____
_____
_____
_____
_____
_____
_____
_____

6. Why is it important to finish what you start, according to the chapter?

_____
_____
_____
_____
_____
_____
_____
_____
_____
_____

7. Why are these moments important for the completion of a destiny?

8. The chapter talks about the "wilderness experience." Why is this experience essential to your personal growth and development?

9. Reflect on a "wilderness experience" that you've gone through. How has it impacted your life?

10. Why is legacy so important? What type of legacy will you leave for those around you?

11. What is the irony of this statement, "Become a graveyard digger"?

12. Consider the puzzle analogy and how it relates to your own life. What "blanks" (any unfinished projects and assignments) could you achieve that will complete your life picture?

Reflective Notes

Chapter 6

Pressing Toward the Goal
(Vision)

"Life is like a jigsaw puzzle, you have to see the whole picture, then put it together piece by piece!"

—Terry McMillian[40]

Terry McMillian's above statement speaks to the very essence of life for me.[40] The reality is that life *is* much like a jigsaw puzzle; and just like a puzzle is put together one piece at a time, pressing toward your goals in life is a one-day-at-a-time process. One of the most important parts of this process is first seeing the finished picture or product, so that you can have a vision for your future.

As I've already shared, my childhood trauma and negative life experiences impeded my ability to see anything for my future beyond unhealthy emotions and life disappointments—at least for a while. When someone doesn't have a vision or picture for life, it's like walking into a pitch-black room and trying to navigate through the darkness.

You will stumble and fall throughout life until you are able to see where you are going. Whenever I walk into a dark room, the first thing that I reach for is the light switch, so that I can see how to navigate and move around the space. When you can't see where you are going in life, life becomes frustrating.

As a kid, I enjoyed putting actual puzzles together. It was fun, and the vision was before me (on the box). Realizing that *life* is a puzzle—one that is not always fun (even though each experience or situation offers its own importance)—is a life-changing revelation. It helps us tie together the pains of the past, the possibilities of the present, and the opportunities of the future…*if* we will stop to identify a vision in which the "pieces" can fit together.

Once you can see where you are going, you will know what pitfalls to avoid and what passage to take in order to pursue success. In professional counseling, I evaluate and assess problematic behaviors with my clients, with the end goal of helping clients to identify behaviors or situations that interfere with achieving mental and emotional wellness. Part of that process is helping my clients to envision themselves overcoming their circumstances. Goal-setting is a highly effective way to create a roadmap to help facilitate the change process to get anywhere you want to go in life.

> *"Better is the end of a thing than its beginning."*
>
> —Ecclesiastes 7:8a (WEB)

What spectacular things are you holding back from the world?
What do you dream about?
What do you talk about?
What do you want to be in life?
What burning desire(s) do you have?

Your God-given potential is limitless!

You are an AMAZING blessing waiting to happen to someone else!

What Goals Are and Are Not

Before setting goals, you need to know what a goal is. A goal is an action plan to set you on the course to actualize your dreams. When setting goals, choose ones that align with your values, so that the goals will be meaningful and of importance.

A goal is:

Your defined vision for your future: Goals should be the result of careful consideration of the things that you want to achieve in your life.

Action-oriented: Goals are meant to be accomplished. When you put action behind your defined vision, two things happen: first, you give vision its needed importance; second, you create a timeframe for achieving the goal. Your actions will determine if the goal should be a short-, mid-, or long-range goal.

Something bigger than you: You are what you think, and, in order to change what you think, you have to think bigger. Don't let F.E.A.R. (False Evidence Appearing Real) stop you from believing that you can achieve your goals in life. The previous chapters of this book were written to get you to think bigger and to pursue your greatness! Set short-, mid-, and long-range goals to achieve your dreams.

A target: You should aim to hit your goals on a regular basis (eg, daily, weekly, or as frequently as possible, according to details surrounding the goals). Remember, short-term goals can become mid- and long-term goals, if they are congruent.

Your goals should not be:

An objective: Your goals describe exactly what you want to achieve. Your objectives identify or list the required actions or steps to achieve your goal. For example, working hard, completing assignments, and getting help as needed are the objectives to the goal of graduating with honors.

Non-specific: When you establish a goal, you have to be specific with what you want to achieve or accomplish. For example, declaring a goal of "losing weight" is non-specific, whereas detailing that "ten pounds will be lost" is very specific—you have established a target to aim for.

Goals can also be divided into different types:

Short-term: These are goals that you set to achieve in a shorter time period. For example, something that you would like to accomplish over the next few days, weeks, or months.

Long-term: These are goals that you plan to accomplish over an extended period of time. For example, these goals span over a period of months or years.

Spiritual: These are goals that target improving your spiritual life with God. For example, reading your Bible daily, praying a certain amount of times a day, and attending church services.

Personal: These are goals aimed at personal growth and development. For example, cultivating certain family dynamics, improving physical health, or engaging in extracurricular activities.

Academic: These are goals aimed at improving your grades in school or level in education; it can include enrolling in academic programs for support.

Professional: These are goals aimed at building your professional skills, enhancing your performance, or expanding your work experience.

Financial: These are goals aimed at saving money, paying off debt, investing, or building your financial portfolio.

Goals are important because they provide personal and professional direction. And once you identify a goal, you can also identify the "why" for pursuing a particular goal in the first place, which can lead to healthy, personal growth, whether your goals are ultimately personal or professional.

Goals help to keep you motivated, because you can track your results (or your progress in reaching them) and make adjustments when necessary. Goals help you identify the picture or finished product that you need or want; and they give you ownership over the process, because you get to both set the goals and the timelines to accomplish them.

The Goal-Setting Process

Goal-setting is the process of identifying something that you want to accomplish. Your goals should be specific, measurable, attainable, relevant, and time-sensitive. This list of attributes is where we get the term SMART goals:

Specific: Make sure that the goal is clear and not vague.[41]

Measurable: You need to be able to measure your success, so that you can track the progression toward your goal.[41]

Achievable: Your goals need to be something that you can reach as well as something within your own control.[41]

Relevant: Your goals should be something that connects or ties into something that is pertinent.[41]

Timely: Your goal should be time related. Keep the goals within a window of time that is neither too far off nor too close.[41]

Using the SMART goal formula will help set you up for success and minimize frustration.

Additionally, here are three things that you want to keep in mind with the goal-setting process:

1. Staying focused on your goals,
2. Staying accountable to your goals, and
3. Staying committed to your goals to get results.

When setting goals, always consider the following:

- What is your reason or your "why" behind desiring a specific goal?
- What is the end product that you would like to see or accomplish? Start with the end in mind.
- Get a vision (picture or image) so that you can see where you are going or what you would like to have. Think about the puzzle analogy. The puzzle's box has the finished product in sight, so that you know what the pieces should look like as a whole once they are joined together.
- When establishing your goals, take into account the things that are important to you, and then build your goals around your values. This approach will help you remain focused, inspired, and have a sense of pride once you obtain your goals.
- Establish goals that you can (reasonably) control. Meaning, your goals should not be dependent on other people or any external factors that are outside of your own decision-making. If it's in your own control, then it's in your own power to accomplish.

Write the Vision and Make It Plain

As you move forward with setting and reaching your goals, review and apply these six steps. While some of these steps may seem basic, it's all part of making the vision plain. And by making it plain, we make it easier to obtain.

Step One: Write down your goals. It's okay to verbalize them to yourself, but it's more effective to write them down, so that you can see and review them regularly as a reminder of where you want to be.

Step Two: Be accountable. Identify an accountability partner to help motivate you and check in on your progress from time to time.

Step Three: Plan for success, not failure. Write down steps that you need to take to achieve your goals. This exercise will help to keep you on track as you work your way through the goal-setting process.

Step Four: Take responsibility. Your goals are not going to automatically happen. Nothing just happens! Put your plan into action, and take it one day at a time.

Step Five: Identify potential barriers. Keep in mind that you will be faced with challenges and frustration along your journey. Make note of these potential barriers, and prepare yourself to face them head on. You can't change what you won't confront. Once you identify your barriers and put strategies in place to confront them, you will feel less intimidated and more comfortable when you encounter the barriers.

Step Six: Be reflective, and make any necessary adjustments. If you don't achieve your goals within the set timeframe, it's okay. It's not the end of the world. Take time to reflect upon and ask yourself the following questions:

- Why didn't I accomplish my goals?
- What changes do I need to make about myself?
- What adjustments or modifications do I need to make regarding my goals?

Self-Reflection & Life Application

Take a moment to consider where you are in life right now and where you would like to be. Ponder what might need to occur to get from "here" to "there," and decide what goals you will aim for.

What is your ultimate goal?

_____
_____
_____
_____
_____
_____
_____

As part of an action plan, write three goals—one short-term, one mid-term, and one long-term—that you want to accomplish in your life.

Short-term goal (one to three months):

_____
_____
_____
_____
_____
_____
_____

Mid-term goal (three to nine months):

_____
_____
_____
_____
_____
_____
_____
_____

Long-term goal (nine months to three years):

_____
_____
_____
_____
_____
_____
_____
_____

On the next page, you will have an opportunity to identify and detail the route to these goals more clearly, including identifying an accountability partner.

Accountability Partner Pledge

Choose an accountability partner who is willing to partner with your progress by checking on you about a certain amount and type of goals. Both of you should write your names below, to reinforce that this is more than a conversation. Rather, it is a commitment.

Briefly name or list the goals that you will be pursuing:

_____

_____

Identify the length of time that you are expecting your accountability partner to be a partner to your progress through accountability:

_____

Accountability partner: _____

Date of partnership: _____ / _____ / _____

Accountability partner: _____

Date of partnership: _____ / _____ / _____

As you begin completing your goals, consistently review, assess, and adjust them.

Use the product goal chart on the next page as a guide to set SMART goals and to stay accountable.

	Description	Action	Follow Up	Date of Completion
P	**Promise to complete the goal.** Make a promise to yourself and others to complete this goal—and stick to it!	Identify the person whom you will allow to hold you accountable to accomplishing your goals.	Decide how often you will follow up with this person.	
R	**Reasonable goals are reachable goals!** Make small achievable goals that lead up to the BIG goal!	Make a list of the smaller goals and deadlines that need to be set to achieve the main goal.	Pick a day of the week to follow up on these goals, mark them as complete as you finish them, and set new ones.	
O	**Open yourself up to making adjustments.** Your goal may change slightly from time to time as you work toward the final product.	Make notation of how you can predict how your goal outcomes may change.	Follow up by the date that you set to see how the goal is progressing as well as how any new insights have impacted it.	
D	**Determination!** The road may get bumpy, but stay determined.	List the ways that you will keep yourself encouraged to accomplish the goal (eg, rewards).	Establish reward dates for meeting your goals.	
U	**Understand** that there is work required!	List the requirements or commitments to obtain this goal.	Follow up on the work that needs to be done on a weekly basis.	
C	**Commitment.**	List the ways that you will keep yourself accountable to your goals.	Check your progress every two weeks. Ask yourself often, "Am I on track?"	
T	**Time management** is the key.	Set timelines to manage your goals.	Beware of time-wasters and distractions that may hinder your forward progress or the completion of your goals.	

The P.R.O.D.U.C.T. goal chart is a tool that is used to identify what you want, to establish a plan to attain what you want, and to set timelines to accomplish what you want.

Read each column of the P.R.O.D.U.C.T. goal chart and follow suggested expectations for each individual goal that you set for yourself.

Suggested Goal Topics

If you're having any trouble identifying what goals to aim for, refresh yourself on the different possibilities by reviewing example categories below.

- **Spiritual goals**
- **Career goals**
- **Financial goals**
- **Educational goals**
- **Relationship goals**

Personal Vision Affirmation

Using the **I.P.D.E.** method, decide where you see yourself in the next three to five years.

- **Identify** the situations and circumstances of your current life.
- **Predict** all the possible outcomes of these situations and circumstances based on your ability to make choices while in them.
- **Decide** on the outcome that you desire most that is also consistent with your ultimate vision for your life.
- **Execute** your decision and commit to "the passage" until you finish the work of bringing this possible outcome to reality, for the purpose of reaching your vision.

What About Me?

Based on your experience of reading *The Passage*, write down five things that you have learned about yourself.

1.

2.

3.

4.

5.

Finish-the-Work Personal Accountability Exercise

Write down five goals or dreams that you attempted to accomplish but, for whatever reason, did not. Decide if these are still goals or dreams that you would like to achieve. For any that you do still want to pursue, set new deadlines for achieving them.

1.
___
___
___
___
___
___
___

Date: /   /

2.
___
___
___
___
___
___
___

Date: /   /

3.

Date: /   /

4.

Date: /   /

5.

Date: /   /

My Plan of Action

The goal I want to achieve is:

_____

_____

Date of finish	How will I measure my success?

Description	Time estimate	Completion date

Obstacles that may arise	How I will respond

Helpful resources

My Plan of Action

The goal I want to achieve is:

_____

_____

Date of finish	How will I measure my success?

Description	Time estimate	Completion date

Obstacles that may arise	How I will respond

Helpful resources

My Plan of Action

The goal I want to achieve is:

_____

_____

Date of finish	How will I measure my success?

Description	Time estimate	Completion date

Obstacles that may arise	How I will respond

Helpful resources

SMART Goals[41]

S	**Specific**	
	What am I going to do? Why is this important to me?	
M	**Measurable**	
	How will I measure my success? How will I know when I have achieved my goal?	
A	**Achievable**	
	What will I do to achieve this goal? How will I accomplish this goal?	
R	**Relevant**	
	Is this goal worthwhile? How will achieving it help me? Does this goal fit my values?	
T	**Timely**	
	When will I accomplish my goal? How long will I give myself?	

Reflective Notes

Salvation

To the millions of people who are seeking love around this world: I give you an open invitation to true love. This love that I'm talking about is a love that forgives, comforts, heals, restores, delivers, protects, preserves, and prospers. This love that I'm talking about gives an unspeakable joy and a peace that surpasses all understanding. This love that I am talking about has a desire to give and never take. The only thing that this love takes away is your sadness, sickness, poverty, pain, and spiritual death. You may be asking yourself, "What kind of love can do this?" The love of God is the love that I'm speaking about. The love of God is the only love that can cover a multitude of sins.

> *"For God so loved the world that He gave His only begotten Son, that whoever believes in Him should not perish but have everlasting life. For God did not send His Son into the world to condemn the world, but that the world through Him might be saved."*
>
> —John 3:16–17 (NKJV)

> *"Therefore if the Son makes you free, you shall be free indeed."*
>
> —John 8:36 (NKJV)

Are you ready to be free?

God has ordained purpose, greatness, and destiny for your life. You have value and worth in the eyes of God! Don't believe the lies of the enemy. Satan wants you to think that you messed up your life so badly that nothing can help you. This is a LIE! The only sin that is unforgiven is the sin that remains unconfessed! It doesn't matter what you did in your past. It doesn't matter how people treat you or view you as a person. The only thing that matters is that God loves you and Jesus paid the price for you to be forgiven and freed from your past! The question is, are you ready to be free? Are you ready to change the course of your life forever?

If your answer is *yes*, then say "Yes" to Jesus today through this prayer of salvation!

Repeat after me on this next page…

Prayer of Salvation

"Dear Lord, I come to you now, just as I am. You know my life and You know how I've lived. I repent of my sin! I ask You to forgive me! Wash me with Your precious blood! I believe that Jesus Christ is the Son of God and that He died for my sin. On the third day, Jesus was raised from the dead. Lord Jesus, I ask You to come into my heart and live Your life in me and through me. Fill my heart with Your love.

I renounce the devil, and I receive Jesus as my new Lord and Savior today! Holy Spirit, have Your way in my life from this day forward. Thank You, Lord, that You have a plan for my life and greatness is my destiny! Lord, keep me forgiven with You and forgiving others, in Jesus's name! Amen."

If you said the words above in sincerity, then I want to personally congratulate you! When you accept Jesus Christ into your heart, all your sins are forgiven. The Bible calls this experience being "born again." This experience is not a natural experience but rather a spiritual one! When you become "born again," it's not an outward change, it's an inward change. Your physical body remains the same. However, your spiritual nature has changed and has become one with God. You are now a new creation in Christ!

"Therefore, if anyone is in Christ, he is a new creation; old things have passed away; behold, all things have become new."

—2 Corinthians 5:17 (NKJV)

Welcome to the family of God!

Endnotes

1. Quote by Alan Kay, "The Best Way to Predict the Future Is to Issue a Press Release," Audrey Watters, November 2, 2016, accessed September 10, 2024, http://hackeducation.com/2016/11/02/futures.

2. Quote by Michael Jordan, "Nike 'Failure' Michael Jordan Ad 1997," Anthony Kalamut, Oct 28, 2019, accessed August 4, 2024, https://www.youtube.com/watch?v=nvrbQBI4ElI.

3. Quote by Winston Churchill, Quotable Quote, Goodreads.com, Goodreads, Inc., accessed September 10, 2024, https://www.goodreads.com/quotes/537399-success-is-the-ability-to-go-from-failure-to-failure.

4. Quote by Abraham Lincoln, "Abraham Lincoln Quotes," BrainyQuote.com, BrainyQuote, accessed September 10, 2024, https://www.brainyquote.com/quotes/abraham_lincoln_109275.

5. "Process," s.v., *American Dictionary of the English Language* (Noah Webster, 1828).

6. Quote by Stephen Covey, "The Habit of Personal Responsibility," The 7 Habits of Highly Effective People: Habit 1: Be Proactive, FranklinCovey-Benelux.com, accessed September 10, 2024, https://www.franklincovey-benelux.com/en/habit-1/#:~:text=Reactive%20people%2C%20on%20the%20other,and%20they%20blame%20the%20weather.

7. Rocky Kanaka, "Watch what happens when I change her name from Venom to Honey," Rocky Kanaka, February 29, 2024, accessed August 4, 2024, https://www.youtube.com/watch?v=M_Vg_yvlFiI.

8. Quote by Winston Churchill, Quotable Quote, Goodreads.com, Goodreads, Inc., accessed September 10, 2024, https://www.goodreads.com/quotes/3270-success-is-not-final-failure-is-not-fatal-it-is.

9. Martin Luther, translated by Dr. John Nicholas Lenker, *Luther's Two Catechisms: Explained by Himself in Six Classic Writings, Book III* (from the Christian Education Book Series), "Lord's Prayer Explained," 305 (The Luther Press: Minneapolis, 1908), accessed August 4, 2024, https://lutherancatechism.com/doc-lib/luther_m_luthers_two_catechisms_explained_by_himself_in_si.pdf.

10. James Strong. "Forsake." In *The New Strong's Expanded Exhaustive Concordance of the Bible*. Nashville: Thomas Nelson, 2010. 5800.

11. Quote by Angela Bassett, Quotefancy.com, Quotefancy, accessed September 6, 2024, https://quotefancy.com/quote/1085023/Angela-Bassett-Don-t-settle-for-average-Bring-your-best-to-the-moment-Then-whether-it.

12. Quote by Myles Munroe, Quotable Quote, Goodreads.com, Goodreads, Inc., accessed September 10, 2024, https://www.goodreads.com/quotes/688275-when-purpose-is-not-known-abuse-is-inevitable.

13. Quote by Steve Jobs, "Steve Jobs Quotes," BrainyQuote.com, BrainyQuote, accessed September 10, 2024, https://www.brainyquote.com/quotes/steve_jobs_126246.

14. Teaching by Bill Winston, Archives, BillWinston.org, Bill Winston Ministries, accessed November 10, 2024, https://www.billwinston.org/archives/.

15. Story of Mariah's Storm, "The Inspiring Tale of Mariah's Storm," HorseRacing.com, accessed September 10, 2024, https://www.horseracing.com/blog/the-inspiring-tale-of-mariahs-storm/.

16. *Merriam-Webster Dictionary*, s.v. "average," *adj.*, accessed November 10, 2024, https://www.merriam-webster.com/dictionary/average.

17. *Merriam-Webster Dictionary*, s.v. "excellent," *adj.*, accessed November 10, 2024, https://www.merriam-webster.com/dictionary/excellent.

18. Gatorade, "Be Like Mike Gatorade Commercial (ORIGINAL)," BigWayne84, accessed November 10, 2024, https://www.youtube.com/watch?v=b0AGiq9j_Ak.

19. Quote by Thomas A. Edison, "Famous Quotes by Thomas Edison," ThomasEdison.org, accessed November 10, 2024, https://www.thomasedison.org/edison-quotes#:~:text=%E2%80%9COpportunity%20is%20missed%20by%20most,overalls%20and%20looks%20like%20work.%E2%80%9D

20. Quote by Lao-Tze, Amor Mundi, "Lao-Tze on How Thoughts Translate into Destiny," Bard, Bard College, July 14, 2015, accessed September 15, 2024. https://hac.bard.edu/amor-mundi/lao-tze-on-how-thoughts-translate-into-destiny-2015-07-14#:~:text=%22Watch%20your%20thoughts%3B%20they%20become,your%20words%3B%20they%20become%20actions.

21. Berry Gordy et al., *The Last Dragon*, Columbia TriStar Home Entertainment, 2001, https://www.youtube.com/watch?v=chiNyErCpAI.

22. Quote by Wade Boggs, "Wade Boggs Quotes," BrainyQuote.com, BrainyQuote, accessed September 15, 2024, https://www.brainyquote.com/quotes/wade_biggs_311616.

23. Quote by Joel Osteen, "Joel Osteen Quotes," BrainyQuote.com, BrainyQuote, accessed September 15, 2024, https://www.brainyquote.com/quotes/joel_osteen_281989.

24. Quote by Raymond Chandler, Quotable Quote, Goodreads.com, Goodreads, Inc., accessed September 15, 2024, https://www.goodreads.com/quotes/1512-ability-is-what-you-re-capable-of-doing-motivation-determines-what.

25. Quote by Brian Tracy, "Brian Tracy Quotes," BrainyQuote.com, BrainyQuote, accessed September 15, 2024, https://www.brainyquote.com/quotes/brain_tracy_125860.

26. Quote by Hilary "Zig" Ziglar, "Zig Ziglar Quotes," BrainyQuote.com, BrainyQuote, accessed September 15, 2024, https://www.brainyquote.com/quotes/zig_ziglar_381975.

27. Quote by Winston Churchill, "Winston Churchill Quotes," BrainyQuote.com, BrainyQuote, accessed September 15, 2024, https://www.brainyquote.com/quotes/winston_churchill_104164.

28. Quote by John C. Maxwell, John Locke, LockeInYourSuccess.com, Locke In Your Success, LLC, September 20, 2008, accessed September 15, 2024, https://www.lockeinyoursuccess.com/the-greatest-day-in-your-life-and-mine-is-when-we-take-total-responsibility-for-our-attitudes-thats-the-day-we-truly-grow-up-john-maxwell-author-and-public-speaker/.

29. Quote by Thomas Jefferson, "Thomas Jefferson Quotes," BrainyQuote.com, BrainyQuote, accessed September 15, 2024, https://www.brainyquote.com/quotes/thomas_jefferson_120994.

30. "Michael Jordan said his high school coach who cut him from the team was also the reason for his resurgent rise - 'He takes pride in that too,' " Siddhant Gupta, Basketball, Sportskeeda, modified April 11, 2023, https://www.sportskeeda.com/basketball/news-michael-jordan-said-high-school-coach-cut-team-also-reason-resurgent-rise-he-takes-pride-too.

31. Quote by John C. Maxwell, Quotable Quote, Goodreads.com, Goodreads, Inc., accessed September 15, 2024, https://www.goodreads.com/quotes/6944013-people-may-hear-your-words-but-they-feel-your-attitude.

32. Quote by Joyce Meyer, "Joyce Meyer Quotes," BrainyQuote.com, BrainyQuote, accessed September 15, 2024, https://www.brainyquote.com/quotes/joyce_meyer_567615.

33. Quote by Hilary "Zig" Ziglar, "Zig Ziglar Quotes," BrainyQuote.com, BrainyQuote, accessed September 15, 2024, https://www.brainyquote.com/quotes/zig_ziglar_617778.

34. Quote by Frederick Douglass, Quotable Quote, Goodreads.com, Goodreads, Inc., accessed September 15, 2024, https://www.goodreads.com/quotes/6398-if-there-is-no-struggle-there-is-no-progress-those.

35. Quote by Richard M. Nixon, "Richard M. Nixon Quotes," BrainyQuote.com, BrainyQuote, accessed September 15, 2024, https://www.brainyquote.com/quotes/richard_m_nixon_402997.

36. Quote by Myles Munroe, Quotable Quote, Goodreads.com, Goodreads, Inc., accessed November 10, 2024, https://www.goodreads.com/quotes/9196732-the-wealthiest-place-in-the-world-is-not-the-gold.

37. Quote by Walter Elliot, "Walter Elliot Quotes," BrainyQuote.com, BrainyQuote, accessed October 5, 2024, https://www.brainyquote.com/quotes/walter_elliot_190719.

38. Quote by Vince Lombardi, "Vince Lombardi Quotes," BrainyQuote.com, BrainyQuote, accessed October 5, 2024, https://www.brainyquote.com/quotes/vince_lombardi_127517.

39. Quote by Gary Gilmore (as credited by Dan Wieden), "Nike's 'Just Do It,' the Last Great Advertising Tagline, Celebrates its 25th Birthday," MDG, LLC, 2024, accessed October 5, 2024, https://www.mdgsolutions.com/learn-about-multi-location-marketing/nikes-just-do-it-the-last-great-advertising-

tagline-celebrates-its-25th-birthday/#:~:text="It%20was%20a%20simple%20 thing,before%20facing%20the%20firing%20squad.

40. Quote by Terry McMillian, Quotable Quote, Goodreads.com, Goodreads, Inc., accessed October 5, 2024, https://www.goodreads.com/quotes/290169-life-is-like-a-jigsaw-puzzle-you-have-to-see.

41. "Everything You Need to Know About SMART Goals," Chelsea Damon, AchieveIt, accessed October 5, 2024, https://www.achieveit.com/resources/blog/everything-you-need-to-know-about-smart-goals/#:~:text=SMART%20 goals%20were%20outlined%20back,organization%20wants%20to%20 move%20forward.

About the Author

T. Dwayne Smith's life journey is rooted in the transformative power of faith, resilience, love, forgiveness, and perseverance. Growing up on the West Side of Chicago and navigating the loss of his parents at a young age, Dwayne learned to channel these values into a lifelong passion for helping others heal, grow, and thrive in life.

As a licensed professional counselor (LPC), school counselor, licensed ordained minister, and life coach, Dwayne has over twenty years of professional experience in mental health, youth development, leadership development, postsecondary support, and career counseling. He is also an active member of the following professional organizations:

- Illinois Counseling Association (ICA)
- Illinois Mental Health Counseling Association (IMHCA)
- Illinois Association of Couple and Family Counselors (IACFC)
- American School Counselor Association (ASCA)
- American Association of Christian Counselors (AACC)

Dwayne's passion is to walk alongside people by encouraging them on their journey toward self-awareness, resilience, spiritual growth, and holistic healing—helping people to develop and build the tools that they need to self-actualize and live more fulfilling and balanced lives.

I WANT TO HEAR FROM YOU!

Book stores and platforms are more likely to promote a work that has received positive reviews. If reading this book gave you a new understanding or benefit in any way, please leave a book review on Amazon to help spread the word and make sure that this message reaches as many people as possible!

Also, feel free to send your written testimony to me at
TDwayne01@gmail.com

Books by T. Dwayne Smith:

The Passage: Navigating Pitfalls on Your Journey to Success

The Process Equals the Product

The Process Equals the Product: Life Application Workbook

I Forgive You: Finding Freedom in Your Darkest Moments

I Forgive You: Finding Freedom in Your Darkest Moments: Workbook and Journal

www.ingramcontent.com/pod-product-compliance
Lightning Source LLC
Chambersburg PA
CBHW070537090426
42735CB00013B/3010